The Expulsion from Gush Katif

THE EXPULSION FROM

GUSH KATIF

EDITED BY NAOMI GROSSMAN

Southern Hills Press

The Expulsion from Gush Katif
www.gushkatifbook.com

Copyright © 2008 by Southern Hills Press. All rights reserved, including the right of reproduction in whole or in part or format. No portion of this book may be utilized in any way or by any means, electronic or mechanical, including photocopying, recording, or any information storage and retrieval system, without permission in writing from the publisher.

The opinions expressed herein are those of the individual authors and do not necessarily represent the views of Southern Hills Press. Southern Hills Press assumes no responsibility for the truth, accuracy, or completeness of any data, views or opinions contained herein. The sole responsibility for the truth, accuracy, completeness, or usefulness of any views, data, or opinions in the content resides with the original authors and Southern Hills Press hereby expressly disclaims any responsibility for the publishing of data, views or opinions of the original authors.

Published by Southern Hills Press, Pittsburgh, PA, USA.
Printed in the United States of America

Cover design: Y. Woolf
The Expulsion from Gush Katif / Southern Hills Press

This book may be ordered through booksellers or by contacting:

Southern Hills Press
PO Box 7074, Jerusalem, 91070, Israel
www.southernhillspress.com

ISBN 978-1-933882-06-2

All Rights Reserved

A Dedication to the People of Gush Katif

*"With my voice, I call to the Lord,
and He answered me
from His holy mount to eternity."*
(Psalms, 3:5)

This book gives a voice to some of the men, women, and children of Gush Katif who, with their very souls, defended the Land of Israel and the right of the Jews to live there.

Their determination and resolution to build their homes and make the desert bloom despite the constant threats under which they lived are an inspiration to us all. And their spirit, faith, and strength, even during the months of heartbreak and devastation since the destruction of their homes, continue to be a light to a weary nation.

It is our most sincere hope that in the near future, they will find their way home.

לשכת הרבנות האזורית "חוף עזה"

יגאל קמינצקי רב חבל קטיף. נווה דקלים ד.נ חוף עזה תובב"א

החונה היום באתר הקרוואנים בניצן 79267 טל 0773010500

There is a famous aphorism from Rav Kook that "remembering is the secret of redemption." Essentially, this means that our ability to correct and improve our ways, and avoid repeating our mistakes in the future depends first and foremost upon our ability to remember and preserve our memories of the past.

The devastation and destruction of Gush Katif was not only a trauma faced by the individuals, families, and communities that were directly affected by this disaster, but it was primarily a national tragedy. When it destroyed and uprooted Gush Katif, the Israeli government effectively destroyed and undermined the basis of faith and idealism that have guided the Jewish nation for generations. With this act of extreme foolishness, the Israeli government first and foremost struck at the land, the nation, the Torah, and the God of Israel. It damaged the mutual responsibility, basic Jewish ethics, and understandings that have characterized the Jewish nation throughout history.

From being "this wise and understanding nation that is this great people," the Israeli government turned us into a "withered and unwise nation." We, the exiles of Gush Katif, are trying to preserve our memory of the past as best we can, and this book can serve as a further reminder and silent witness of the atrocity and crime that the Israeli government committed against its citizens and people.

I would like to express my appreciation to Southern Hills for publishing this important work that will, God willing, help to open the eyes of the blind and reveal their erroneous ways.

With great blessings,
Yigal Kaminetsky
Chief Rabbi of Gush Katif

לשכת הרבנות האזורית "חוף עזה"

יגאל קמינצקי רב חבל קטיף. נווה דקלים ד.נ חוף עזה תובב"א

החונה היום באתר הקרוואנים בניצן 79267 טל 0773010500

ישנה אימרה מפורסמת של הרב קוק: "בזכירה סוד הגאולה", שמשמעותה היא שהיכולת שלנו לתקן ולהיטיב את דרכינו, ולמנוע הישנותן של שגיאות אלו בעתיד, תלויה בראש וראשונה ביכולת לזכור ולשמר את זיכרון העבר.

חורבן והרס גוש קטיף הינו טראומה לא רק ברמה הפרטית של יחידים, משפחות, וקהילות שחוו אסון זה, אלא הוא בראש וראשונה טרגדיה לאומית. ממשלת ישראל, בחורבן ועקירת גוש קטיף, הרסה וקעקעה את בסיס האמונה והאידיאלים שעם ישראל הלך לאורם דורות רבים. במעשה נואל זה בעטה ממשלת ישראל והעומד בראשה, בארץ ישראל, בעם ישראל, בתורת ישראל, באלוקי ישראל, בערבות ההדדית, במוסר היהודי הבסיסי, בתבונה היהודית ועוד, שאפיינו את עם ישראל לדורותיו.

מ"עם חכם ונבון הגוי הגדול הזה" הפכה אותנו ממשלת ישראל ל"עם נבל ולא חכם"

אנחנו עקורי גוש קטיף משתדלים לשמר את זיכרון העבר ככל יכולתנו, וספר זה יכול לשמש נדבך נוסף בזיכרון זה ועדות אילמת לעוול ולפשע שפעלה ממשלת ישראל כלפי בניה וכלפי עמה.

יישר כוח גדול לסדרן היילס פרס על הוצאת חומר חשוב זה שבע"ה יסייע לפקוח עיני עיוורים ולהאיר של דרכם של טועים.

בברכת התורה והארץ
יגאל קמינצקי
רב גוש קטיף תובב"א

Member of the Knesset
Binyamin Elon

The Expulsion from Gush Katif sums up a tragic time in Jewish history, when Israeli citizens were removed from their homes by their own government. Ariel Sharon's Disengagement Plan will live on in Israeli collective memory, and its scars on the delicate fabric of Israeli society are as yet unknown.

The summer of 2005, when the expulsion occurred, will always be remembered for its orange flags, demonstrations, tears, hopes, and dashed dreams. *The Expulsion from Gush Katif* captures the spirit of that summer and the aspirations of the residents of Jewish Gaza both before and after the Disengagement Plan. Its moving essays and diaries ensure that the importance and significance of the events described are not lost to future generations and Jews around the world.

Benny Elon, MK
Chairman of the Ichud Leumi

Thank G-d for this book which exposes the betrayal and unkept promises of the Israeli government to the wonderful, hardworking Jews of Gush Katif. Rabbi Elnekaveh makes us painfully aware of the continuing human rights disaster many of these families are enduring with respect to lack of employment, family relations, housing, and schooling.

Shame on the Israeli government and Jewish leaders for igniting this situation of their brothers and sisters and allowing it to continue. Jews regularly cry out for the difficult plights of non-Jews around the world but remain silent on the Jews of Gaza.

The devastating reality that this book portrays will inspire more of us to fight the appeasement insanity of giving more holy Jewish land to an Arab terrorist, anti-Semitic regime and to fight the appeasement insanity of forcibly evicting more Jewish families from their homes in Judea and Samaria. It will also help rouse us to speak out on behalf of the Jews of Gaza to alleviate their unconscionable living conditions.

The phrase "never again" has been used in various contexts by Jews. This important book makes it an imperative that must also "never again" allow what happened to the Jews of Gaza to happen to the Jews of Judea and Samaria.

Mortimer Klein
National President Zionist Organization of America

Member of the Knesset
Prof. Arieh Eldad

The Disengagement Plan, which led to the expulsion of thousands of Israeli civilians from their homes in Gush Katif and northern Samaria during the summer of 2005, was a turning point in Israeli history. Most of us will never forget the harrowing photographs of people being dragged from their homes or the demolition of public buildings and private homes.

The Expulsion from Gush Katif is a vivid chronicle of those events, told from a variety of perspectives. It gives the reader a moving, realistic view of what it was like to live under the threat of being removed from one's home, as well as the actual expulsion, and the events that followed.

I recommend this book to anyone who wants to understand the tragic, life-changing events of that summer and the resultant effects that it has had upon Israeli society.

I recommend this book for everyone, in order to prevent such events in the future.

Prof. Arieh Eldad, MK

Contents

Acknowledgements   1

Foreword   3

A Map of Israel and the Surrounding Region   5
A Map of Modern Day Israel   6
A Map of the Gaza Region   7
Settlements and Population of Gush Katif Before the Expulsion   8

Introduction

A History of Jewish Life in the Gaza Strip   9
    By Sara Bedein

Jewish Gaza in More Modern Times   15
    By Sara Bedein

The Expulsion from Gush Katif and the Situation Today   20
    By Naomi Grossman

Section One: Recollection of Life in Jewish Gaza Before the Expulsion

Living on a Prayer   27
    By Rabbi Yosef Elnekaveh

The Tunnels and the Kissufim Route   29
    By Rabbi Yosef Elnekaveh

A Short Visit to Three Katif Communities   33
   By Paula R. Stern

Money Won't Tempt Us   36
   By Ami Shaked and Yehudit Tayar

Life As a Resident of Gush Katif –   39
Mayan's Story
   By Sara Yocheved Rigler

The Story of Roz and Paul Schneid –   44
A Visit to Gaza
   By Naomi Ragen

130,000 in Human Chain from Gush Katif   56
to Jerusalem
   By Tovah Lazaroff and Matthew Gutman

The Prayer of the Sixty Thousand   61
   By Rabbi Yosef Elnekaveh

From the Diary of a Former Gaza Resident   66
   By Dr. Pesach Aceman

Diaries of the Last Days of Gush Katif   70
   By Toby Klein Greenwald

A Diary With No Title   82
   By Chaim Gibber

Section Two: Expulsion and Desecration

The Walls That Had the Last Word   91
   Photos Provided by Debbie Rosen

Contents

A Personal Recollection of the Expulsion from Gush Katif By Zimra Siegman-Schlessinger	96
"A Barbaric Act" – The Destruction of the Synagogues in Gush Katif By Ali Waked	109
The Story of Roz and Paul Schneid, Part Two – Homeless and Wandering By Naomi Ragen	112
A Synagogue or a Bathroom? By Paula R. Stern	116
And Even the Dead – To Unbury a Son By Rachel Saperstein	122
The Day of the Expulsion Photos Provided by Debbie Rosen	127

Section Three: The Aftermath

The Aftermath Photos Provided by Debbie Rosen	139
After the Expulsion By Rabbi Yosef Elnekaveh	143
My Neighbor from Bombay By Shifra Shomron	145
Gush Katif Revisited By Esther Marcus	148

And We Know Not What to Do…   155
  By Rabbi Yosef Elnekaveh

The Spirit of Gush Katif: Don't Let it Get   158
Washed Away
  By Judy Lash Balint

Gaza's Best-Kept Secrets   165
  By Michael Freund

From Golden Stalks to Golden Grains and   169
Back Again
  By Shifra Shomron

The Service of the Heart   172
  By Rabbi Yosef Elnekaveh

Section Four: Reports on Life After the Disengagement

Betrayal, Broken Hearts, and Pain Remain   177
the Legacy of Ex-Gazans
  By Toby Klein Greenwald

Forgotten Refugees   183
  By Rachel Ginsberg

Israeli Teen Refugees Attempt Suicide,   202
Drop Out
  By Aaron Klein

Thirty Years in Thirty Minutes   205
  By Anita Tucker

CONTENTS

The Displaced Jews of Gush Katif: 209
Twenty Months Without a Home
  By Hillel Fendel

About the Authors   219

Glossary of Terms   225

Acknowledgements

This book would not have come about without the help and guidance of so many. We would like to express our deepest thanks to all those who assisted in bringing this work to fruition.

To all those who contributed their work. Without your contributions and stories, there wouldn't be a book. It is a brave and difficult process to write one's own experiences, especially when they are wrought with so much pain; but sharing allows others to gain an invaluable insight and we are grateful to you for this: Dr. Pesach Aceman, Judy Lash Balint, Sara Bedein, Rabbi Yosef Elnekaveh, Hillel Fendel, Chaim Gibber, Rachel Ginsberg, Matthew Gutman, Aaron Klein, Tova Lazaroff, Esther Marcus, Pinchas Orbach, Naomi Ragen, Sara Yocheved Rigler, Rachel Saperstein, Ami Shaked Shifra Shomron, Zimra Siegman-Schlessinger, Yehudit Tayar, Anita Tucker, and Ali Waked. Particular thanks must be given to Michael Freund, Douglas Goldstein, Toby Klein Greenwald, Debbie Rosen, and Paula R. Stern for their invaluable advice, time, work, and input.

To Naomi Grossman for translating and editing this book. To Yaffa Schoffman for copyediting. To Shira Rachel Adelman, Rhoda Goldstein, Abby Hazony, and Miriyam Kampf for proofreading. To Henry Valier for the layout, and to Yitz Woolf for his skills, talent, and perseverance in designing the cover.

To *The Jerusalem Post*, *Moment Magazine*, Israel National News, Koret Communications, aish.com, *Mishpacha Magazine*, World Net Daily, *Cleveland Jewish News*, and Ynet News for providing resources and information.

To all the additional people who provided their support and input in countless ways, particularly: Simon Bengen, Naomi Klein, Katy Last, Yoram Ohana, Ashley Sevitz, Caroline Wilson, and Alicia Zur-Spiro. There are too many to list individually, but the response and support we have received for this book, and the help, care, and energies that people put forth to help bring it into existence have been phenomenal.

Thanks also go to The People of Israel who reached out to the Jews of Gaza, before, during, and after The Expulsion, with physical, emotional, and financial support. Without your help, the situation of Gush Katif's Jews would not be the same. With your help, their story will continue to be told and their lives rebuilt.

Emma Lazarus
Southern Hills Press

Please note: Style and spelling may vary among the different entries due to our desire to retain the individual style of each author.

Foreword

In the summer of 2005, a noble chapter in the history of Jewish settlement in the Holy Land was closed when the Israeli government carried out its "Disengagement Plan," forcibly evacuating thousands of Jewish residents from the Gush Katif bloc, a group of agricultural communities in the Gaza Strip. The residents were dragged from their homes, which were then demolished and razed to the ground, bringing 35 years of modern settlement in the area to an end.

Gaza is first mentioned in the Torah, where it was promised to the descendants of our ancestors Avraham, Yitzchak, and Yaakov. Jews have lived in the area for centuries, since Talmudic times, and despite several expulsions they have always returned.

In modern times, the Jews "made the desert bloom" in Gaza, building up the Gush Katif bloc into what became the breadbasket of Israel. With government help, Jews established thriving communities in Gush Katif during the 1970s. Despite suffering many acts of Arab terror over the years, these brave Jews were determined to stay in their homes and create a beautiful heritage for their children. Over time, they built up a flourishing greenhouse industry, which developed into a major part of Israel's agricultural exports. Gush Katif's flowers, fruit, and vegetables, and especially its bug-free lettuce, became known around the world for their high quality.

One of the saddest parts of the events of 2005 is that this was the first expulsion order in history to be carried out by Jews, against Jews. Despite the negative effects that the Disengagement Plan would have on the economy, as well as on the region's security, the plan was ruthlessly executed. Even the dead were not allowed to remain behind. Within a few weeks, years of toil, love, and dreams were reduced to a pile of rubble, and thousands of upright, hardworking Israeli citizens had become homeless refugees.

The purpose of this book is to make sure that the memories of Jewish life in Gush Katif will never fade, or become yet another historical fact to forget. For those of us who never lived in Gush Katif or even had the opportunity to visit the area, it is hard to believe that it was once a thriving group of communities with an active life of its own. This book tells the tragic story of the summer of 2005, including the events leading up to the expulsion, as well as its aftermath. At the same time, it gives a voice to some of the other players in this drama, the brave men and women who lived and built their lives there, only to see their hopes and aspirations torn down so tragically.

The summer of 2005, with its orange banners, demonstrations, hopes, and disappointments, should never be forgotten. For the former residents of Gush Katif, the dream will never die, and they look forward to when they will return. By reading this book, let us share and understand that dream.

Naomi Grossman
Editor

A Map of Israel and the Surrounding Region

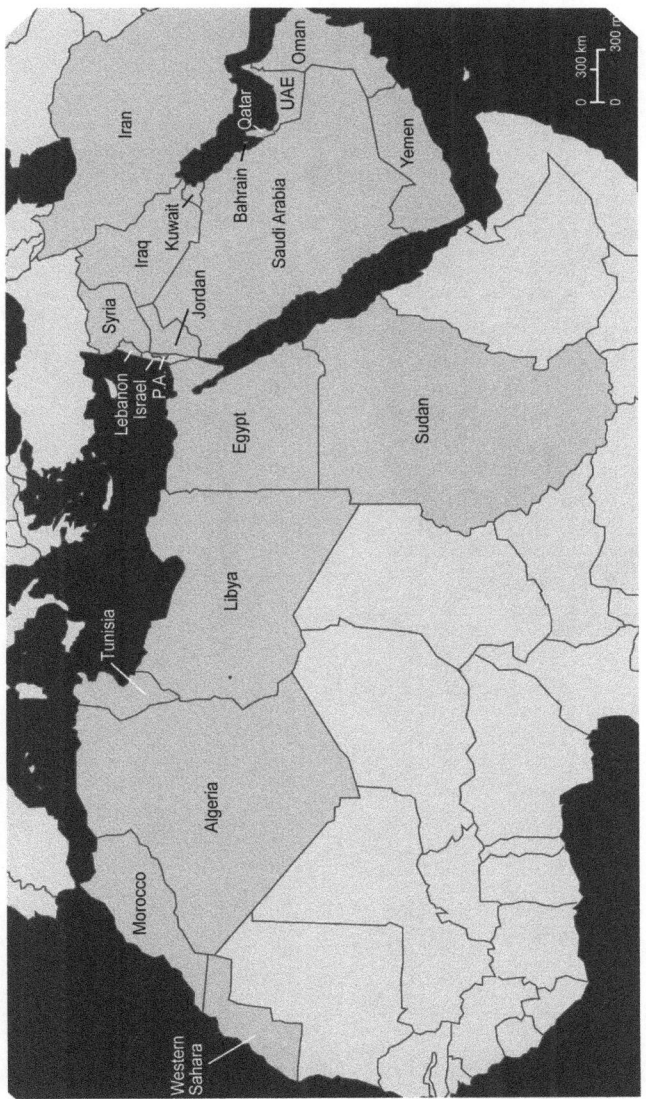

Map provided by Koret Communications, www.koret.com

A Map of Modern Day Israel

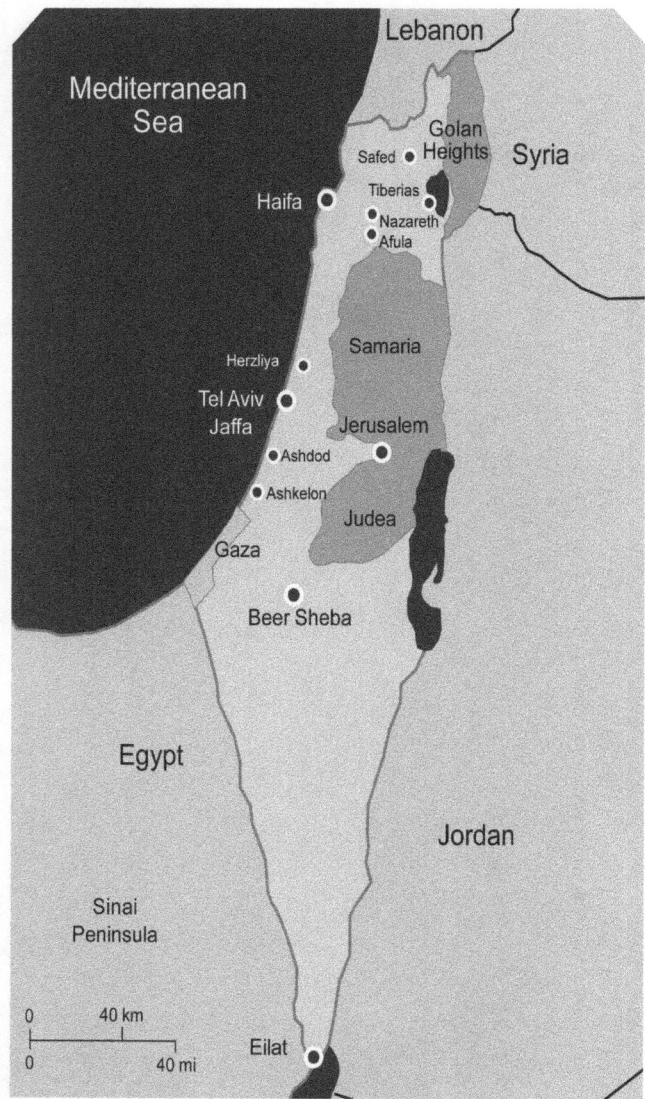

Map provided by Koret Communications, www.koret.com

A Map of the Gaza Region

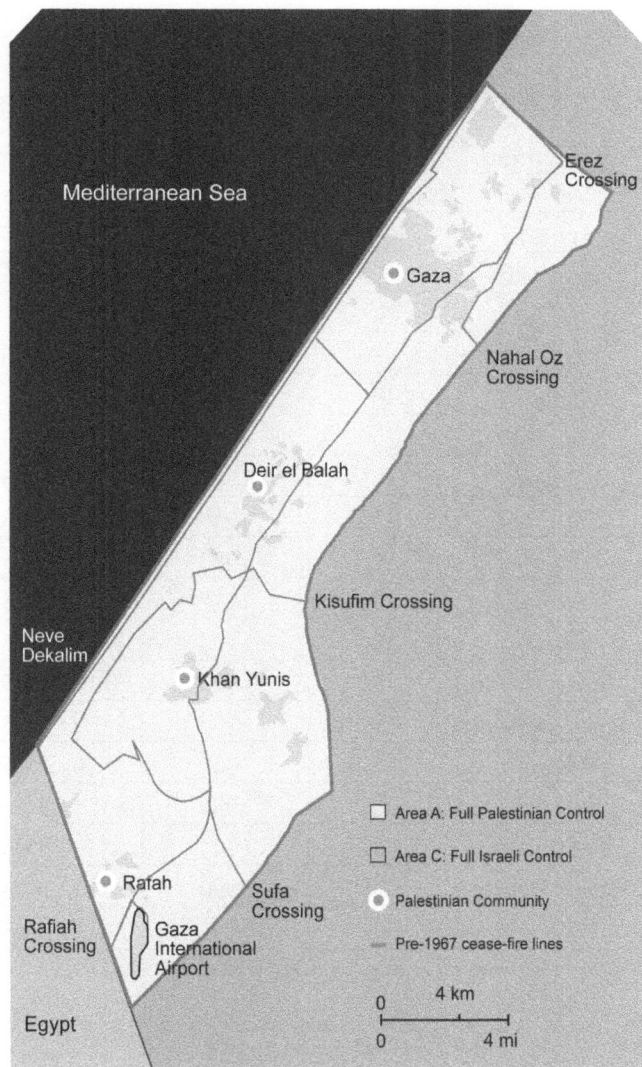

Map provided by Koret Communications, www.koret.com

Settlements and Population of Gush Katif Before the Expulsion

Settlement	Population	Date Established	Date of Evacuation
Alei Sinai	350	1983	8/21/2005
Atzmona	650	1982	8/21/2005
Bedolach	220	1986	8/17/2005
Dugit	80	1982	8/16/2005
Gadid	310	1982	8/19/2005
Ganei Tal	400	1973	8/17/2005
Gan Or	350	1983	8/19/2005
Katif	405	1985	8/21/2005
Kfar Darom	365	1989	8/19/2005
Kfar Yam	20	1983	8/19/2005
Morag	220	1972	8/17/2005
Netzarim	390	1972	8/22/2005
Netzer Hazani	410	1973	8/19/2005
Neve Dekalim	2,500	1983	8/19/2005
Nissanit	1,050	1980	8/16/2005
Pe'at Sade	105	1989	8/16/2005
Rafah Yam	150	1984	8/16/2005
Shirat Hayam	50	2000	8/19/2005
Tel Katifa	75	1992	8/17/2005

© Koret Communications, www.israelinsider.com/dmap

Introduction

A History of Jewish Life in the Gaza Strip
By Sara Bedein

Every Israeli school child learns that "the river of Egypt" (*Bereishit* 15:18), i.e., the eastern tributary of the Nile, is the border of the biblical Land of Israel. (Even if someone claims that this is Wadi El Arish, it is still west of Gaza.) Whoever has learned any history knows that our forefathers, the Hasmoneans, and the Sages of the Mishnah and Talmud were there, and that Rabbi Ovadiah of Bartenura and Rabbi Meshulam of Volterra described Jewish communities there. Moreover, Rabbi Yisrael Najara, while serving as Rabbi of Gaza, wrote the *Ka Ribon Olam* liturgical melody sung on Shabbat. Only in the 1929 riots were the Jews removed from the Gaza Strip. After the Six Day War, many Jews returned to the area, and by the time the Sharon government expelled them from their homes in 2005, over 8,000 Jewish men, women, and children were living in Gush Katif. Prior to the expulsion, the Gazan communities were the breadbasket of Israel, contributing around $40 million to the Israeli economy.

The earliest mention of Gaza in the Torah occurs in *Bereishit* 10:19, where it is described as the southern terminus of the land of Canaan. The Phoenicians, a sea-faring people from Crete, had begun to settle in the area during the time of Avraham and, in later centuries, developed a powerful confederacy that was dominated by their five principal cities, which included not only Gaza, but also Ashkelon, Gat, Ekron, and Ashdod. These kingdoms lasted until the reigns of David and Shlomo.

This territory, like the rest of the Holy Land, was promised by God to our forefathers, Avraham, Yitzchak, and Yaakov. Avraham and Yitzchak lived in the Gaza Strip region. Chapter 26 of *Bereishit* describes how, due to a famine in the land, Yitzchak went to the city of Gerar, located in the Gaza Strip, where Avimelech, king of the Philistines, resided. It is written: "The Lord then appeared to him and said: 'Do not go down to Egypt; settle in the land which I shall point out to you. Reside as a stranger in this land and I will be with you and bless you; for to you and your descendants I will give all these regions, and so fulfill the oath which I made to your father Avraham...I will give your descendants this whole country.'" (26:2-4). Then in 26:6: "So Yitzchak settled in Gerar."

In the time of Yehoshua, "Gaza with her towns and villages unto the River of Egypt and the Great Sea" (located today around El Arish) (*Yehoshua* 15:47) was allotted to the tribe of Yehudah. It was the scene of Shimshon slaying the Philistines in the Temple of Dagon. Shlomo conquered Gaza, which by then contained a mixed gentile population, making it part of the southern limits of the Kingdom of Israel. Centuries later, it would trade in slaves with Edom, a practice that the Prophet Amos fiercely condemned.

In the Talmudic period, Gaza was a pagan city, but the local Jews turned it into a center of Talmud. Soon, other communities sprang up in the surrounding area, until Talmudic centers were established in the towns and villages stretching from Rafiach (today called "Rafah" by the Arabs) to Yavneh. In 508 BCE, a synagogue was built in Gaza, attracting pilgrims from all over Israel and the Diaspora. Remnants of that synagogue can still be found today in Gaza City. According to the 10th century Karaite scholar Sahl ben Matzliah, Gaza was one of the three cities in the Land of Israel that served as a place of pilgrimage (the others being Tiberias and Zoar).

Yonatan the Hasmonean (the brother of Yehudah the Maccabi) succeeded in conquering Gaza and settling there in 145 BCE, and his brother Shimon, who developed the Jewish settlement there, states in *The Book of Maccabees* (1:15) "Not a strange land we have conquered, and not over the possessions of strangers we have ruled, but of the inheritance of our Fathers that was in the hands of the enemy for some time and was conquered unlawfully, and as for us, when we had the chance – we returned on to ourselves the inheritance of our Fathers."

Byzantine rule, which began shortly after the beginning of the Talmudic period, was very harsh toward the Jews, but the communities of Gaza and Rafiach flourished. With the Arab invasion in the 7th century, the Jews of Gaza actually fought alongside the Byzantines. However, the Arabs took it in 634 CE and, as the first Arab settlers began to migrate to Palestine as a whole, so did they settle in Gaza. Gaza and Rafiach continued to thrive under Arab rule, although the surrounding communities began to decline.

Gaza became a center of Jewish learning under a certain Rav Moshe. The Spanish linguist, Dunash ben Labrat, lived there for a time, and during the 11th century, rabbi Ephraim went from Gaza to the important Rabbinical community of Fostat in Egypt.

The Crusader invasion in 1099, under their King Baldwin III, destroyed the community in Gaza (although visitors still described one there) and most of the surrounding area. The mixed gentile populations were also driven out, with the exception of the Christians. But the Jews in Rafiach managed to survive the onslaughts, and this city even served as a place of refuge for Jews fleeing Crusader atrocities elsewhere. But during the later Crusader period even Rafiach was abandoned.

The Mamelukes of Egypt conquered Israel in 1291, and in the 14th century the Jewish community of Gaza revived. Arabs also came to settle in the town, which soon contained an Arab majority. This was a comparatively peaceful period. Gaza grew and achieved some level of prosperity. The cultivation of wine and raising of cereals were occupations in which the local Jews engaged. The city also became one of the important centers for the Samaritan community, along with Jaffa, Tulkarem, and certainly Shechem. Over the years, however, they migrated to other parts of Israel and the Levant, and the community dwindled once again.

In the 15th century, the Mameluke authorities in Palestine began to oppress the Jews with a heavy burden of taxes, as well as other types of social restrictions. Sometimes, the Arabs joined in the oppression. Jerusalem was hit harder than any other city in the country. At this time, Gaza, and sometimes Hebron, began to serve as a place of refuge for Jews fleeing from the oppression of the authorities. What was Jerusalem's loss became Gaza's gain, and by the

1480s the community prospered under its Chief Rabbi, Moshe of Prague.

The Ottoman conquest in 1516 benefited the Jews of Gaza, and even Rafiach briefly revived. For centuries, the Rabbis of Jerusalem debated whether Gaza and the surrounding area were part of the Land of Israel according to Jewish law. This same debate also centered around Jaffa, Haifa, and Acre. However, the Rabbis must have ruled in Gaza's favor, as the local farm owners were obligated to observe the Biblical laws of agriculture — laws that could be applied only within the borders of Israel.

Among the many Jewish individuals who have visited, or lived in, Gaza since the Ottoman conquest are:

- David Reubeni, a false messiah who claimed to be a representative of a Jewish kingdom in Arabia. In 1523, he visited Jerusalem and also preached the coming redemption to the Gazan Jews.
- Najara, a prominent Rabbinic family from Damascus that settled in Gaza in the 16th century and contributed to the local Rabbinate. Yisrael ben Moshe Najara, author of the work *Zemirot Yisrael*, was Gaza's Chief Rabbi and president of the tribunal in the middle of the 17th century. He was buried in Gaza and was succeeded by his son, Moshe Najara II.
- Rabbi Avraham Eliakim, a respected Gazan Rabbi who lived there around 1601. In 1619, a plague broke out in Hebron, forcing many Jews to seek refuge in Gaza as well as Jerusalem.

- Eliezer Arha, one of the Hebron refugees, who was so revered by the community that he became Gaza's Chief Rabbi.
- Kabbalistic author and commentator, Rabbi Avraham Azulai of Fez, also from Hebron, who wrote his mystical work *Chessed l'Avraham* in Gaza. He later returned to Hebron, where he died.
- Samuel ben David, a Karaite scholar who, during his pilgrimage to Palestine in 1641, visited Gaza and described the community in detail.
- Nathan Ghazzati, a mystic. He was a native of Jerusalem and son-in-law of a rich and pious German Jew, Elisha Halevi Ha'ashkenazi. A fanatical kabbalist, he convinced the mystic Shabtai Zvi that he was the messiah, thus starting a movement that later became known as Shabbateanism. Gaza was the center of this movement and Nathan proclaimed it to be the new capital of Israel. He died in Sofia.
- Rav Tzedakah, a 17th century Rabbinic scholar.
- Castel, a prominent Rabbinic family that settled in Palestine shortly after the expulsion from Spain in 1492. They soon settled in Gaza and, like the Najaras, the Castels became the ruling Rabbinical family there throughout the 18th century. They were also skilled craftsmen. Avraham Castel was Gaza's Chief Rabbi during Napoleon's invasion of the country in 1799. In contemporary history, the artist Moshe Castel was a descendant of this family.

Jewish Gaza in More Modern Times
By Sara Bedein

With Napoleon's invasion, Gaza was the first place to fall. Napoleon had been known to be a friend to the Jews and he invaded Palestine in order to reestablish the Jewish state. But the Jews were not convinced of his actions and reports from Gaza noted the terrible abuse that the local Jews suffered at the hands of the French soldiers, at times joined by the local Arabs, who had, long ago, become more fanatical. The Jews, therefore, fled in numbers, mostly to Hebron. Some Jews remained in Gaza for several more years, but owing to continued Arab persecution, even they fled, settling in Jerusalem. By the first decade of the 19th century, the old Jewish community had vanished. Several years later, the Arabs expelled the small Samaritan community. From that time until the late 1870s, no Jew or Samaritan would dare live in the city. The area from the River of Egypt to Jaffa was given over to swamps, Arab marauders, and bandits.

At the close of the 1870s, a group of Jews managed to settle in Gaza. They were, in the main, barley merchants who traded with the Bedouins for grain, which they then sold to the breweries in Europe. But the presence of a reestablished Jewish community bothered the Arabs, and in 1890 the Jews of Gaza became the victims of a blood libel. In that year, a couple of local Jews employed an Arab boy as a servant. One day, the boy was playing with another Arab boy who owned a camel. Unfortunately, they both had guns, a custom in Arab society, and tragically, the servant accidentally killed his playmate.

Almost immediately, the victim's next of kin killed the servant.

Shortly afterwards, the Jews informed a Turkish judicial tribunal in Jerusalem of the incident. But due to intense propaganda from the local Arabs, the authorities became convinced of the age-old belief that Jews needed gentile blood for Passover and that the Jews had killed the boy. The Jews were arrested and thrown in jail. This caused an international incident because the accused were under foreign protection, as were so many other Palestinian Jews at that time. To ease the situation, the authorities immediately set them free, prompting the Arabs to then force the Turks to restrict Jewish immigration to any part of Israel. Arab immigration, on the other hand, continued unhindered.

An attempt to revive the Jewish community of Rafiach occurred between 1905 and 1913, when Jewish leaders and institutions tried to purchase land in and around the town. (The same occurred in Khan Yunis, which in the 1930s had a Jewish population of three.) However, these attempts all failed due to legal considerations and Arab hostility. In 1920 and 1921, many Jews fled Gaza after anti-Jewish rioting by Arabs. In the 1929 riots, the rest were driven from their homes, and thereafter the Arabs banned Jews from living there. The ancient synagogue was used as part of a mosque and the Jewish cemetery was used as a garbage dump. This is the situation to this day. The community was now dispersed throughout Palestine, but they made their contributions to Israeli society. For example, Marcel Liebowitz, a native of Gaza, became a successful film distributor in the

1930s, working with local and international film companies.

Due to the British military presence and the accompanying employment opportunities, Arab immigrants poured into the area, as they did the rest of Palestine, without any hindrance. Such immigration continued until the War of Independence.

By 1946, a Jewish group succeeded in renewing the Jewish presence in the area and outside the Arab-populated neighborhoods. They purchased a plot of land that became the kibbutz of Kfar Darom, built on top of the ancient Jewish town of Darom that flourished in the Talmudic era. After the 7th century Arab conquest, this site was renamed Deir, later lengthened to Deir-el-Balah.

Rafiach had a sinister revival at this time. With the struggle against the British after World War II, many Jews were arrested and, along with Acre, Rafiach served as a prison camp for Jewish leaders, as well as for soldiers of the Jewish groups that fought for independence, including the Haganah, Irgun, and Lehi. During the War of Independence, the Jews of Kfar Darom were expelled, as were the few Jews who lived in Khan Yunis. A story was told of one Abu Ish, *mukhtar* of a neighboring Arab village, who had gone to Gaza City on business. An Arab Muslim, he was a descendant of 7th century Jewish refugees from Arabia. Because of his ancestry, and because of his village's good relations with the Jews, he was accused of being a Zionist spy and, without any trial or investigation, was promptly hanged in the public square.

Toward the end of the war, the entire area was conquered by Egypt and it soon became known as the Gaza Strip. Arab refugees, for which Israel was not the cause, swelled in population. Indeed, Israel was busy fighting for survival and, at the same time, caring for the Jewish refugees from Europe and neighboring Arab countries. Between the end of the War of Independence in 1948 and the beginning of the Six Day War in 1967, Jews were banned from entering the Gaza Strip. Instead, the place was used as a springboard for raids by the *fedayeen*, Arab guerillas, that often attacked Jewish civilians. The Suez Campaign of 1956, in spite of its international condemnation, stopped all that with Israel's recapture of the Strip. The international community forced Israel to relinquish the Strip the next year – a mistake that would come back to haunt it 10 years later.

In 1967, due to a massive Arab build-up on its borders, Israel made a preemptive strike, thus saving itself from annihilation. All historic Jewish land was back in Israel's hands within a week, after a 19 year separation. Gaza City was still off-limits to Jews (a ban that exists to this day), but three years after the war, Kfar Darom was reestablished. It is located in the area called the "River of Gerar," where our forefathers Avraham, Yitzchak, and Yaakov resided. The place is referred to in the Talmud as a Jewish settlement. About 70 years ago, a Jewish citrus grower by the name of Tuvia Miller purchased 260 dunams of land in the area. In 1945, The National Jewish Fund purchased the land from Miller and settled a group of Jews there in 1946. During the War of Independence, a brave battle was waged between the Kfar Darom Jews and the Arabs. The local Jews were able to fend off the Egyptian army for three months, thus affording precious time for the fledgling Israeli army to get organized to protect the heart of the country.

" ...We knew that if Kfar Darom would not be able to fend off the enemy, and the enemy would reach Yad Mordechai, then Tel Aviv would be under immediate danger... and only history will know to appreciate properly the tremendous contribution and sacrifice made by the residents of Kfar Darom in the War of Independence..." (Moshe Netzer, commander of the second regiment of the Palmach).

This time, the Jews were determined to keep their long and historic presence in the area, and by the end of the 1970s, three more communities were established – Netzer Chazani, Atzmona, and Ganei Tal.

Eventually, 25 communities were established in the area, centered around the Gush Katif bloc, without harming the local Arabs. In fact, before the first intifada in 1987, Jews and Arabs in the area mixed more or less freely; security permitting, Jews visited the Arab cities, and the Arabs were often employed by the local Jewish communities. When the intifada broke out, all that changed, although many Arabs were still employed by the Jews. After the signing of the Oslo Accords in 1993, the Gazan Jews were threatened, once again, with expulsion. When the second intifada broke out in 2000, all contact between Arabs and Jews was cut off completely. Afterwards, the local Jews had to put up with gunfire and bombs directed at them, as well as over 4,000 Kassam rocket attacks against their communities.

The Expulsion from Gush Katif and the Situation Today
By Naomi Grossman

In August 2005, the Jews of the Gaza Strip were expelled from their homes and communities as a result of then-Prime Minister Ariel Sharon's Disengagement Plan. This was the fourth expulsion of Jews from the area since 1920, but the only time that such a banishment was ever carried out by Jews. Despite many protests, prayer gatherings, and petitions both in Israel and abroad to halt the plan, Sharon was determined to expel the Jewish residents from the Gaza Strip.

On August 17th, 2005, just three days after the fast of Tisha B'Av (9th Av), which commemorates the destruction of both Temples in Jerusalem and the descent of the Jewish nation into exile, IDF soldiers and policemen began evicting the residents of the 25 communities of Gush Katif from their homes. Not a single household, synagogue, study hall, school, or business was allowed to remain. Even the dead were removed from their graves and reburied in other cemeteries around Israel, despite the wishes of many of the families of the deceased.

It took only several weeks to dismantle and raze what had been flourishing Torah and agricultural communities that had grown up over a period of 35 years. The 1,667 families that gave them life were forcibly removed, first to hotels and then to temporary "caravilla" sites. It was a very long time before many of them received any of the compensation or temporary housing originally promised by the Disengagement Administration (SELA) and its head, Yonatan Bassi. As of April 1st, 2007, 405 of these families are still living together in 26 temporary sites. Not one permanent home has begun to be built, despite government promises (Hillel Fendel, Arutz Sheva, "The Displaced Jews of Gush Katif: 20 Months Without a Home").

The full effects of the expulsion from Gush Katif, both on those who were removed from their homes and on the young soldiers who had to carry out this unpleasant mission, still remain to be seen. Before the Disengagement, the Gush Katif towns were pleasant places to live, with thriving local industries and educational institutions. A report by the Gush Katif Residents' Committee, published in April 2007, now tells a sadly different story:

Unemployment was almost unknown in Gush Katif, yet 20 months after the expulsion, joblessness stands at 37 percent.

The displaced families face hardships and psychological pressures caused by financial difficulties, forced unemployment, an uncertain future, loss of their community and friends, tight living quarters, bureaucracy, and the like.

The financial compensation provided by the government for new housing is being used by some of the displaced families for day-to-day living. Only 30 percent of the families have received the full amount, but almost all have been given partial compensation.

However, the indomitable community spirit of the Gush Katif residents lives on. As stated in the actual report, "The communities of Gush Katif are a paradigm of mutual responsibility and concern for the collective. Most of the expellees have remained in some sort of a communal framework, hoping to perpetuate their values, ideals, and vision that existed in Gush Katif. Their support for each other is something to be admired."

This book provides an account of life in Gush Katif during the run-up to the Disengagement, the expulsion, and its aftermath. Various personal accounts of those dramatic days, including personal diaries, newspaper reports, and eyewitness accounts, are reproduced here, giving the reader a varied record of these events from many different angles and points of view.

From here, the reader can re-live Gush Katif, The Disengagement, and its aftermath with those brave pioneers. We hope that those who "made the desert bloom" will one day continue to cultivate the deserts of Israel and their stories will not be forgotten.

Section One:

Recollections of Life in Jewish Gaza Before the Expulsion

Living on a Prayer
By Rabbi Yosef Elnekaveh

One of the most amazing miracles that occurred in Gush Katif was the way in which its residents survived constant bombardments from mortars and Kassam rockets. Thousands of missiles of various types were launched at us over the years. In fact, there was even a neighborhood in Neve Dekalim that was named after the mortars that fell there due to its proximity to the Arab town of Khan Yunis, from where many of these missiles were launched.

In one of the suburbs of Khan Yunis, near the shore, a certain mosque remained standing even after the IDF had destroyed all of the surrounding houses from where many of these missiles had been launched. The terrorists used this mosque as a secure hiding place for their weapons, knowing that the Jews would never dare destroy a place of worship.

Several years ago, I told the area commander that terrorists were using a grove of fruit-bearing trees opposite Kfar Darom to shield them as they shot at Israeli vehicles driving along the nearby road. When a division commander arrived in the area to view the situation, the security officers showed him the terrorists' hiding place. With a wry smile, the division commander asked, "What should be done?"

I told him that it is written in the Torah that we should not destroy trees, because "man is a tree of the field." A tree of the field that people use with respect and derive benefit from should remain. However, when terrorists are using a tree of the field to carry out their acts of murder it should not be left standing.

The division commander accordingly ordered the members of the field engineering squad to clear the area of anything that would create a danger on this road.

I therefore used the same logic to approach the division commander again, telling him that a mosque should only be allowed to remain standing if it is actually used for prayer. But when a mosque is used as a shelter for murderers, its *muftis* incite its worshippers to kill, and shots are fired from within its boundaries, it should be destroyed.

Unfortunately, it was not so easy to put my recommendations into action this time. The mosque remained standing, and the terrorists continued to fire mortars from it unceasingly every single night.

But it is God who watches over the guardians of His land, rather than the flesh-and-blood government, who did not restrain the enemy and let them continue to use a place of worship as a tool for murder and destruction in their god's name.

Over the years, there were so many open miracles that they almost became a part of the order of nature.

For example, when a missile landed at the home of the Ezriel family, the explosion resounded throughout the area. The house trembled and the missile made a small hole in the iron doorpost before stopping…right next to the mezuzah.

Our Guardian does not slumber, but continues to guard the doorposts of Israel.

The Tunnels and the Kissufim Route
By Rabbi Yosef Elnekaveh

On more than one occasion, I heard from soldiers serving in the Gaza Strip that while they were on guard duty near a tower called the Filbus, they heard the noise of digging, and it sounded as if a tunnel was being excavated.

I immediately spoke with the local intelligence officer and the intelligence officer for Southern Command. To my surprise, they told me that they had received similar reports and complaints about this issue.

In my innocence, I had always thought that whenever there was any suspicion of digging, the army would carry out searches for tunnels and the soldiers would be redeployed to cover dangerous positions. But the situation carried on as usual, without any change.

After several soldiers approached me again, I met personally with the intelligence officer of the brigade serving in the Gaza Strip. He confirmed that the incident was under investigation. Sounds had indeed been heard, and the matter was in hand.

At this point, I began to wonder if I was crazy. Such clear information had been received and the fact that it had come from several sources was enough to erase any doubts. Yet nothing concrete was being done about the situation. So I immediately approached Defense Minister Shaul Mofaz. A meeting was scheduled and the day before it was due to take place he announced on the radio that Gaza did not belong to the Jews.

Accordingly, I put the following day's meeting to good use. I opened *Yehoshua* and showed Mofaz where it describes the first Biblical conquest of Gaza by the *Bnei Yisrael*. I explained to him at length the amazing history of the Gaza Strip. In fact, after Mofaz received other complaints from local residents, he retracted his statement and said that Gaza really is Jewish land.

During the same meeting, we discussed security. I said that no one had ever thought that the short Kissufim route that cuts inward would be the cause of so much bloodshed, and we moved on to the issue of the tunnels.

Before this meeting, I had been in touch with the Technion, asking if there was machinery that could reveal the existence of tunnels. I understood that such an item may exist, and that it could be developed. However, the cost of such equipment was very high.

I mentioned this to the minister, and we talked about the tunnels and what the soldiers had heard. Unfortunately, nothing changed, and I am not surprised at all today when I hear about various subsequent incidents connected with the tunnels, such as the abduction of IDF soldier Cpl. Gilad Shalit. Even now, the Israeli government and security forces should be doing whatever they can to be sure that there are no tunnels, and they should create the infrastructure that would prevent such construction from taking place.

When it came to the issue of our security, we did whatever we could to improve our safety, while constantly liaising with the authorities. Therefore, whenever harsh statements were made against our settlement of the land, we were not afraid to respond in kind.

Various statements that I made regarding security and the reasons for terror attacks were broadcast on one particular radio program. Below is a transcript of the interview:

> "Our blood is no less red than that of the residents of the Sharon Valley and Ariel. Gush Katif is our home," said Rabbi Yosef Elnekaveh, Chief Rabbi of Gush Katif, in an interview with the show *Sogrim Yom* [The End of the Day].
>
> The Rabbi said that he condemns what appears to be the inability of the State of Israel and its "sophisticated army," to use his term, to prevent attacks on a six-kilometer strip of road.
>
> "Since the attack in Kfar Darom," says Rabbi Elnekaveh, "we have issued warnings that this is a dangerous strip of road that is not patrolled enough. We cannot believe that the State of Israel is unable to erect a separation fence between us and Deir-el-Balah."
>
> Rabbi Elnekaveh also reacted to Minister Gideon Ezra's statements in a recent media interview by saying that he should be put on trial. "I am calling upon the Movement for Fairness in Government to demand that Gideon Ezra resign from the Israeli government," he said. Rabbi Elnekaveh was referring to an interview with Gideon Ezra about a tragic incident in which an entire family was murdered in Gush Katif and, "instead of giving words of comfort, [Ezra] said, 'I told them that that's what would happen if you don't leave the Gaza Strip. Because the residents of Gush Katif are living there, this is why

such disasters have happened, and therefore we need to disengage from there."

Rabbi Elnekaveh added that a short time after these statements were made, Ezra stated that he was very concerned, following the response of those among the Likud party who advocated settlement, that the Disengagement Plan might be shelved.

"I was at the polls, and I saw the residents of Gush Katif and their families there. They should be ashamed of themselves. They don't belong to the Likud. They do not interest us, and tomorrow they'll go home. Who allowed them to go to the polls in the first place? We don't need them. Let them go to their own parties," Ezra noted.

Rabbi Elnekaveh's response was, "I would like to let Gideon Ezra know that many Likud members live in the Gush, and if anyone needs to go home, it's him. We will ask him to resign from the Israeli government, or that he should be fired immediately. Anyone who speaks like that about the families of Gush Katif has no right to sit in the Israeli government."

A Short Visit to Three Gush Katif Communities
By Paula R. Stern

This article appeared in www.paulasays.com. Its original title was "A Tour of Gush Katif."

Before I first visited Gush Katif, I wondered how it was possible to grow anything in sand. There's a technical answer having to do with fertilizers, computerized watering systems, greenhouses that shield the tender plants from the harsh sun, and more. But beyond the technical answer is a deeper one — a love of the land, a will to grow, a need to build.

Netzer Chazani

The thriving, agricultural town of Netzer Chazani was the first civilian community built in Gush Katif. Constructed in the early 1970s, with the encouragement of the Ministry of Agriculture, it was even named after a former Agriculture Minister, the late Michael Chazani. The community is made up of about 70 families, and it is a fine example of how the Jews of Gush Katif have "made the desert bloom." Most people living here earn their living from growing flowers, vegetables, and herbs, mostly from greenhouses that they built up themselves. These products are widely sold, both at home and abroad.

A famous story is told about the beginning of this beautiful community that throws a different light upon the relationship between the Jews of Gush Katif and their Arab neighbors. Soon after its first residents arrived, they were astonished to receive a visit from the mayor of the Arab town of Khan Yunis. The mayor welcomed them warmly with the traditional greeting of bread and salt, and told them that he was happy they had come. He explained that the land was "cursed" and that nothing had grown there from the time of Avraham, forefather of the Jews and the Arabs. Now that the Jews had returned to the land, the mayor explained, it would once again yield food and with it, employment for his people. It is incredible how right he was.

At the entrance to Netzer Chazani stands a memorial to Tali Hatuel and her girls. Tali and little Hila, Hadar, Roni, and baby Merav were murdered on May 2, 2004 by Palestinian terrorists. The brutality of their murder should shock the world. Their memorial service, which was interrupted by gunfire as the mourners themselves were attacked, was especially difficult to watch. In their memory, the people of Gush Katif built a resting place for the soldiers who protect them.

Neve Dekalim

Unlike most of the settlements in Gush Katif, Neve Dekalim is not agriculture-based. The town features an amazing zoo, a shopping center, community center, wonderful parks, lush lawns, and beautiful homes.

Over 500 families live in Neve Dekalim, Gush Katif's largest town, which was founded in 1983. Its schools are famous for their high standard of education, attracting children from throughout Gush Katif. They include day-care centers and kindergartens, an elementary school, and an *ulpana* (religious dormitory high school for girls). Adult education facilities exist here too, including several yeshivot, a women's college, a community center, a research center for the study of the Sinai region, and a youth center. Neve Dekalim even has a successful Golden Agers' Club, catering to the needs of the region's older residents. Neve Dekalim's growing size is reflected in its eight synagogues, regional library, two medical clinics, and a commercial center boasting many and varied shops.

One of the most amazing places in Neve Dekalim is the children's zoo. It is an oasis of grass and life and peace for the animals, for the children of Neve Dekalim, and for all visitors lucky enough to attend.

Atzmona

Further to the south of Neve Dekalim lies the beautiful town of Atzmona. Though it is smaller in size, it is also quite lovely. The homes are gracious, the lawns maintained well. Atzmona has many greenhouses. We visited an incredible plant nursery. The quality of the plants, the careful way they were organized and cared for, was easy to see. We left with a trunk full of plants for incredible prices.

Money Won't Tempt Us
By Ami Shaked and Yehudit Tayar

Printed in The Jerusalem Post.

on May 25, 2005

We, the Jewish people, have an unusual, unbreakable connection to our land that has lasted through the long, endless generations of the Diaspora and persecution.

We, who live in Yesha, [Judea, Samaria, and Gaza], understand the connection of our people to our land more than many of our brethren in other areas of Israel. However, it was this same spirit of connecting the people and the land that encouraged the pioneers who drained the swamps in Galilee and faced danger and disease and now, in our generation, has us determined to stay in the hills and valleys and shores of our beloved homeland.

We, through our spirit of fortitude, have turned empty wasteland, barren hills, and virgin sand dunes into a Garden of Eden. We have paid in sweat and blood and created towns, built communities, and planted fields. We are determined to continue in this direction and protect the birthright of the Jewish people – our land.

Who came up with the idea that if they give us money we would consent to leave our homes? The people of Gush Katif realize that taking such money would destroy the community spirit we have built here.

For 30 years we have built here together as a community – and we have become even more than a family. If we were to take money to leave, we would be destroying the glorious community that we have achieved.

Prime Minister Ariel Sharon did not appreciate the extent of our commitment. He took it for granted that by now a mere 20 percent of us would still be here. The opposite is true. One hundred percent of us are here and plan to stay. We are still in our homes and fields and plan to remain here.

Our refusal to take money sends a message to the people of Israel. So Sharon intends to banish us from our homes and from our communities and turn our lives upside down....

In Gaza we are farmers; we toil the land and our lives are ordered in accordance with the agricultural needs of our land. What is important to us is our land, our families, and our community. Those who mistakenly thought it possible to translate this into money have been proven wrong. For 30 years we have lived among the Arabs and have surpassed them in our connection to and development of the land. With determination and fortitude, and despite the heavy price we pay, we have succeeded.

We who personally deal with security – with life and death situations – have made it clear to our residents that anyone who translates our lives here into money is hurting the sacred memory of our fallen and the honor and dignity of our injured. He is hurting all of the people who are working in Gush Katif's security division night and day to save human lives.

We will do all that we can to maintain this ideal combination of people and land. Our struggle is a moral and righteous one against the decision of a passing government to destroy the lives of over 2,000 families and the irreplaceable legacy of the connection of the people of Israel and the Land of Israel.

One of the most infuriating aspects of this whole plan is the fact that its implementation will not bring peace and quiet and will not bring security to the people of Israel. On the contrary, it will bring terror into Ashkelon, Shaar Hanegev, Netivot, and other areas. These regions have no security infrastructure to deal with the prospects of terror as we know it, nor do the populations have the fortitude to live under the terror as we do.

We believe in our inalienable right as the nation of Israel to protect our birthright; no amount of money will tempt us to destroy our lives or jeopardize the future of the people of Israel.

In May 1966, David Ben-Gurion wrote: "People of the Earth, brave in action, and aware in conscience …shine….in incomparable human glory and historical depth…Future generations will be able to draw on the spirit of our pioneers, their faith in their own capacities, and their knowledge that the great historic labors of our times, and the objectives imposed upon our people, are still at their very beginnings."

Life As a Resident of Gush Katif – Mayan's Story
By Sara Yocheved Rigler

This article originally appeared in www.aish.com, a leading Judaism website.

Mayan was born far from the Zionist dream, into a Catholic family in Yugoslavia. Until the age of ten, her childhood was one of peace and affluence, ski trips, and boating vacations. Then her father died. Two years later, war broke out. "This war turned me, suddenly, into a 'Croatian,' the evil enemy of my best friends, who, I now discovered, were 'Serbians.'"

Caught during the war in a Serbian-occupied area, Mayan, her mother, and her sister endured five years of hunger, cold, and the deaths of their friends. They struggled to survive, motivated by their "firm belief in Croatian unity and nationalism" and their hopes to rejoin their own people. Finally, through hard work, they managed to buy passports to escape to the Croatian side of the border.

They were greeted by nothing. "When we reached our 'promised land,' nobody there cared; there was no support and no help for us." Seventeen-year-old Mayan felt betrayed by her own people. "Everything in my life was unreliable and false. I felt a compulsion that I must start my life all over again from the very beginning."

A few years later, Mayan took a job as a waitress on a ship. There she met Eyal Yadai, the ship's Israeli security officer. Mayan accompanied Eyal back to Israel, but he told her that he would not marry her unless she converted to Judaism. Mayan now decided to learn about Judaism. "I gladly began to learn the details of this new way of life that I had yearned for, the life of a nation where all really care about each other with devotion," she recalls.

Several months later, as her conversion neared, Mayan told Eyal that she would marry only a man who was religious. So Eyal, too, began studying Judaism. They finally married as two observant Jews.

In 2003, they moved to the settlement of Netzer Chazani in Gush Katif. That very day, Eyal had to report for his month-long reserve duty. Mayan was left alone in their tiny, rented house with their one-year-old daughter. She was a 26-year-old foreigner, pregnant, and knew no one in Netzer Chazani. Suddenly there was a knock on the door. She opened it to find a smiling neighbor with a loaf of fresh bread. Soon, another knock. Another neighbor had come with a home-cooked meal. Then another knock: a neighbor was inviting her for a Shabbat meal. "I was never left alone for the entire month."

Mayan was overwhelmed by her welcome. In the words of a *mishnah* that Mayan loves to quote: "All Jews are responsible one for the other."

Test of Fire

Three months later, their test of fire came. As Eyal, Mayan, and their daughter, Avia, were driving out of Gush Katif, they suddenly saw two Arabs with automatic rifles on the road in front of them running straight toward their car. The Arabs started shooting at them. Eyal floored the accelerator. Five bullets penetrated the Yadais' car. "Each bullet," asserts

Mayan, "was a personal miracle to each member of my family, missing each of us by millimeters."

They made it to the Israeli army outpost at the Kissufim Crossing, a few hundred meters away. The gunfire continued, as soldiers from the outpost raced to the scene. The terrorists managed to kill Tali Hatuel, eight months pregnant, who was driving the car behind the Yadais. When the Hatuel car stopped, the terrorists approached it and fired close-range at Tali's four young daughters, murdering all of them, including the toddler strapped into her car seat.

The Yadais were still at the outpost, trembling from their near-miss, when one of the soldiers returned, weeping. "I killed one of the terrorists," he sobbed, "but I was two minutes too late to save the children."

They had been on their way elsewhere, but Eyal and Mayan, in their bullet-riddled car, drove directly to the Western Wall in Jerusalem to thank God for their lives.

In the wake of this terror attack, the residents of Netzer Chazani told the Yadais that they would understand if they left Gush Katif. They knew it was not easy to live like this. Mayan replied, "What? With wonderful neighbors like you, I can be strong and I can stay here forever. Especially now, leaving is not an option." The community supported them. "For one month after the attack, we did not eat one meal alone. Our fellow Jews came to be with us."

Unity in Gush Katif

"To tell you how much people are united here, in Netzer Chazani there is one synagogue where everyone prays together – Sephardim, Ashkenazim, Moroccans, Yemenites. Here you can find Jews from every nation, and no one looks down on anyone. You can see how they pray together – no arguing, never, never. There's real harmony here."

"I will go with these people to the ends of the earth," Mayan declares. "The people here are so amazing, so soft, so nice. Now they have become fighters because they don't have a choice, but that's not their nature. I look at the way they raise their children, and that's the way I want to raise my children. I pray with all my heart that I'll stay here for many years to come."

Mayan says that a visit to Gush Katif causes many to change their minds about the Disengagement. "People start to see more than what they see in the news....I have not met one person who didn't change his mind after seeing Gush Katif. Only when you see this beautiful, blossoming, flourishing place can you understand.

"They see that we are normal people, that we don't have vampire teeth, that we have normal homes and normal kids and normal education, that we don't teach our kids to hate. They don't even know that we live in normal houses. They think we live in trailers; they expect to see me, a mother carrying a gun, with dirty, sandy children beside me. Once two people from the government came. At 2:00 in the afternoon, they said, 'It's getting late. Let's go to Gush Katif.' I said, 'This *is* Gush Katif.' They couldn't believe me."

What Plans has Mayan Made for the Disengagement?

"I don't think about the day of the expulsion. I don't even know the date. I live in a rented house, so I'll get nothing. And I don't want anything. But if it happens, I have nowhere to go. The only place I can go is the Western Wall. And there you'll find me. It's my second home. If God doesn't want me here, I'll be there, in His home. And that, too, will be for the best. But, until the end, I'm going to fight."

How Does This Young Mother Fight?

"I use the explanation of my life to make people understand better how important the Land of Israel is, and how important it is to me. Today I have a stable home, and I don't want to lose it. And prayer is the strongest weapon. If God heard the prayer of a young girl in a small Croatian town, then He will certainly listen to the prayers of His People living in their homeland."

The Story of Roz and Paul Schneid – A Visit to Gaza
By Naomi Ragen

This article first appeared in Moment Magazine.

We are on our way from Jerusalem to Netzer Chazani, a Jewish settlement in the Gaza Strip, to meet Roz and Paul Schneid at their farm. They have lived there, growing flowers, lettuce, and tomatoes in sand in huge hot-houses, for the last 27 years. If the Israeli government's Disengagement Plan goes through, as most Israelis believe it will, the Schneids are set to be deported, forcibly if necessary, in August, 2005. We want to know what they are planning to do, and how they feel about the radical political changes that are sweeping over the country like tidal waves. I am the first journalist Roz and Paul have agreed to speak to since a very traumatic experience they had with Thomas Friedman of the *The New York Times* several years back, when he interviewed them and later wrote what they felt was a very distorted and negative piece in which he compared their home to a "castle" amid the poverty-stricken Arabs of Gaza. I look around at the very modest little house, the kind the Jewish Agency built for new immigrants 30 years ago, and ask: "When did you move out of the castle?" They laugh.

We have known each other for over 30 years, having met in the spanking Jewish Agency apartment blocks that sprouted like mushrooms in the hills of Jerusalem during the years following the Six Day War.

Roz, 58, was born and raised in New Bedford, Massachusetts. Paul, 60, was born in Manhattan, part of a large Rabbinical family on his mother's side. After getting to know each other in America, they were married in Israel in 1968, giving Roz's family their first trip there. They returned to America, but soon made plans to leave permanently. Roz was 22 and Paul was 24. Eventually, they landed in Jerusalem, as did we. I remember those days after the Six Day War – the raw neighborhoods full of building materials and the smell of new paint, the rides to Arab villages to buy fruits and vegetables and household items for bargain prices, the friendly interchanges with Arab workers, to whom we gave boxes of American candies and who graciously reciprocated with huge bunches of grapes from their home orchards.

Like the rest of us Western immigrants, the Schneids soon found white-collar jobs: Roz taught English (which she says she hated) and Paul found work as one of the editors of *Encyclopedia Judaica*, later becoming the head of Keter Publishing House's Judaica department. Their lives soon fell into a busy routine. But something was missing. "We were living life by rote," Paul remembers. Roz, especially, needed more to feed her restless pioneering spirit.

At first they didn't want to go too far afield from Jerusalem; they didn't want to get their hands dirty. After a failed attempt at settling in a communal settlement named Moshav Elazar in Gush Etzion, they looked north, to Israel's beautiful, green Galilee. "But when we went to the Jewish Agency, they told us: 'Don't go there! All the settlements in the Galilee are failing.'" So instead, they looked South. Their friends Anita and Steve Tucker were already living in Netzer

Chazani, one of the first ten families sent by the Jewish Agency to settle what at the time Israel considered strategically vital Jewish outposts in the Gaza Strip, known as Gush Katif, annexed by Israel when Egypt lost the Six Day War. The land was no prize.

Acres and acres of sandy, infertile soil with no infrastructure.

"Anita was trying very hard to start a school there, because her kids were traveling really long distances every morning. But they needed 21 kids to get the funding. So they asked us to register our four to help them out." Even though they were all pre-schoolers, Roz registered them all, including the one she was still pregnant with. "But then, on the way home, we thought: "This is really not very honest. If we've registered our children here, we should live here. So, we thought: Why not? It was as good as anywhere else. We'll live there until it's not good anymore."

"That was 27 years ago," Paul says. "We were given two *dunams* of land and a little three-bedroom house." They were the 22nd family in the entire area. Everything was covered with sand. In fact, on their first visit, their car got stuck in a dune. The Jewish Agency hired an expert in experimental hot-house farming, an immigrant from New Zealand, to teach them what to do with their land. "He didn't speak a word of Hebrew, so he taught me all he knew, and I translated it into Hebrew and taught the others. And this is how I became the big expert on growing tomatoes," Paul laughs. In time, Paul even volunteered to teach the Palestinians in Gaza the same farming methods. They repaid him by stealing his equipment.

It was a good life, despite the fact that they rose at seven and went to bed at two or three in the morning. "In publishing, you are always on some cut-throat deadline. Everybody is always yelling. Here, all I have to do is argue with plants. And they don't argue back."

Roz admits she loves it. "It's what I always wanted to do," she says. It hurts her that she doesn't have energy for a home garden.

"We're getting older," Paul admits. He looks tired.

The Disengagement has come at a particularly inopportune time for Paul Schneid. This past February, he was diagnosed with colon cancer. He has already endured one operation, chemotherapy, and radiation to reduce his tumor. He had more surgery in June and then five months of chemotherapy. Earlier this year, he had a hip replacement. He doesn't look like a farmer, with his medium build and Rabbinical beard. His friendly blue eyes that light up when something amuses or angers him are bloodshot. Economically, farming has had its ups and downs. "We once picked 35,000 flowers in one day and got such a low price, we would have made more money if we hadn't grown them at all," he remembers. "The flowers were terrible," Roz agrees.

"Every year, the biggest crop was always ready just as I was doing my Passover cleaning. And every year, we almost got divorced over it! But then there was the year that one week's worth of cherry tomatoes, some six tons, just happened to come to market at the highest prices, making them a windfall equal to two years' profit."

Paul was one of the first to grow organic cherry tomatoes and strawberries in Israel. And all of Gush

Katif is known for its bug-free greens, especially prized by Orthodox Jews who otherwise need to hand-check every leaf carefully. Europe, which used to be the main market for Israel's agricultural exports, recently considered laws heavily taxing produce grown in Jewish settlements. Before that, there was an unofficial boycott. Paul, who was once in charge of planning all organic hot-house growing in Israel for Agrexco, Israel's produce exporting union, has long stopped growing for export to Europe. "I don't want to deal with them," he says without rancor. When I compare farming to gambling in Las Vegas, Paul shakes his head. "In farming, at least God is involved. You put the seed in the ground. He decides what will come of it."

I look around me. It's a small, welcoming house, nothing at all like the luxurious one-family Mediterranean villas that have been sprouting up all over Israel for the last decade. The furniture is lived-in and comfortable – a few chairs, a couch, a coffee table. The sign on their front door is chipped and the door itself could use a coat of varnish. The Schneids, it is clear, have not spent their lives making money, but spending it modestly to raise their large family. The walls are decorated with family pictures of the couple's eight children and 13 grandchildren. They have seven sons and a daughter. Five are married. Five of their sons are in the army, four of them holding high-ranking posts as career army officers. Their only daughter, Naomi, is a gynecologist at Soroka Hospital in Beersheva. She is married to a general practitioner, and the mother of three. The Schneids' children live in places like Jerusalem, and in small settlements in the Southern Hebron hills. Their two youngest are still in yeshiva, the same one attended by all their brothers: Netiv Meir in Jerusalem, one of the most prestigious in the country.

How do their children feel about the Disengagement, especially the ones in the army? "Some of them are angry. One wants to quit the army. And another one thinks it might be good," she shrugs. That none of their children want to take over the hot-houses is fine with Paul and Roz. "We want them to do whatever makes them happy. Besides, I don't need their help running the hot-houses. I can do it myself. I can hire workers. The hot-houses are my pension. It's all I've got."

The hot-houses are a three-minute drive from the house. Ever since an ax attack against a farmer by one of his Arab workers, the hot-houses have been separated by barbed wire from the residences of Netzar Chazani. The dull, gray plastic stretched over metal frames looks like plane hangars that could hold an entire air force. There are hundreds of them, each filled with parsley, or mint, or spinach, or tomatoes, all growing in sand under the hot sun. The sight that awaits us when we pull back the gray plastic sheets weighted with wood to keep out the insects, is breathtaking. We are suddenly in a green oasis, with acres and acres of ripe, full lettuce ready for picking – 56,000 of them in one hot-house alone.

Paul has five such hot-houses together with his partner, where plants are watered and fed by sophisticated drip irrigation systems that seem nothing less than miraculous. He leans down and picks a few, cutting off the dark roots, and removing a few leaves, saying a special prayer. According to Torah law, all produce grown in the land of Israel must have tithes set aside for the poor. While some Rabbis have said that these laws don't apply to Gush Katif, Paul disagrees. He quotes the verse from *Bereishit*, "And Yitzchak dwelt in Gerar many years." He points outside. "This is Gerar. This is where our ancestors came from." I imagine how many thousands of tons of fresh produce are growing in this spot, how many tax dollars they bring in, and how, come August, it will all be destroyed.

Paul walks ahead, bending down to examine a whole new area of seedlings that have just been planted. Is he continuing his work, regardless? "It's not going to happen," he repeats, as he does each time I broach the subject. Roz, who is involved in the local school, echoes his sentiments. "We are planning our curriculum for next year. Nothing has changed."

A strong breeze makes the metal frame shake. Paul looks up sharply, disturbed. "It's only the wind, honey," Roz assures him. I too feel a shiver. We are all alone, surrounded by acres of deserted hothouses, our only companions the silent growth all around, in a place where just over the fence terrorist groups train, bomb factories produce mortars and suicide belts, and horrible tragedies have become part of daily life. No man, woman, or child in Gush Katif, whatever the age, has been given immunity. Less than a year ago, all of Israel was shocked by the murder of Tali Hatuel and her four little girls. I ask them about what it's been like all these years, dealing with the security problems, and why they put themselves through it.

"When we moved here, there wasn't even a question. Arab caravans with camels passed by our front door every day. There were no fences at all. The Arabs in Khan Yunis even opened up a mini-market that carried kosher food for us. My daughter got her first glasses in Khan Yunis. We bought our vegetables there, had our car fixed, hired our workers there. We were good customers, good neighbors. The Bedouin used the dried-out tomato plants for building their huts and for animal feed, and at the end of each growing season, we'd help them to load the plants onto our tractor and we'd transport it out to their tents. One year, the woman asked if Roz could come along. So we all went. When we got there, we unloaded the plants and she invited Roz in. She said I couldn't come because her husband wasn't there." She had a breakfront full of the cleanest cut glass in the middle of all that sand," Roz remembers. "When we gave back Yamit to the Egyptians (as part of the King David accords between Sadat and Begin in 1979) all the Bedouin were given cards telling them which side of the border of Rafiach they were on – Israeli or Egyptian. She got the Egyptian side and she was heartbroken. One day she came to me and asked if I would let Paul take another wife. She offered us her daughter. That way, they'd be able to stay near us."

"But for some reason, Roz didn't think that was a good idea," Paul says dryly.

"Days before the evacuation, they brought us huge boxes of candies for the kids and they cried and cried and cried. Now our workers are terrified that they are all going to be fired if the Disengagement takes place."

"Who are your workers, where do they come from?" I ask.

"They're our neighbors," he gestures to the houses just beyond the wall put up to keep out sniper fire. Gush Katif's settlers give employment to thousands of Gazan Arabs. Paul employs seven. But how does he know who to hire, after all? The hot-houses are so soundless, so isolated. "We hire members of the same families. A brother, a cousin, of someone who has been a good worker. They are also screened by the army, who has to give them work permits." Off the record, Paul also tells me a story that indicates that the Israeli army has precise intelligence on every terrorist working out of Gaza.

When did the real security problems begin? "It was 1986. One of our neighbors was shopping in the Khan Yunis market when he was stabbed in the back. It shocked everyone, because it happened just out of the blue." Shortly after that, the Schneids and the rest of Gush Katif's Jewish settlers stopped shopping there. The peace accords between Israel and Egypt and the expulsion of Jewish settlers from Yamit led to a deterioration in relations between Arabs and Jews in the area. "We had to take turns being watchmen, because we were afraid of terrorist infiltration. People from Yamit would say to us: 'When are you moving?' Or, 'Why are you building since obviously you're next?' I thought it was a joke. I guess for us Yamit was like what Gush Katif is for the rest of the country: it was way down South. It was far away."

Every year, security worsened. A farmer was axed by his worker. A few years later, this same man's wife was shot in their car when the couple was on their way to a wedding. Two years ago, the settlement's Rabbi was in his car with his wife and six children when terrorists opened fire. Three hundred shells were found outside the pockmarked car, but only one penetrated. "It went through the back of the Rabbi's seat and through his heart." Paul's voice breaks. "He was a great Torah scholar."

And then there was the time when their 11-year-old son went out the back door and ran back in, shouting, "They're shooting at me!" So Roz told him, "Go out the front door," Paul shakes his head. Only two months ago, Roz went out to clean her front porch. Paul was in the synagogue saying his morning prayers. When she came back into the kitchen and sat down to drink her morning coffee, the sky suddenly opened up, raining big globs of dirt on the kitchen window. By the time she realized a mortar shell had fallen in their front yard, it was all over. "It's amazing how you can learn to live with almost anything," they tell me. "How it doesn't lessen at all your resolve to stay."

"You are sitting here in the middle of all of this. What are you thinking?" I ask them. Roz takes a while to answer me. "The Arabs can do whatever they want to do, but it won't change the fact that this is my land and I'm living on it. I'm not talking personally. I mean it's my nation's land. It's land that was given to the Jewish people, and we have every right to be here."

I try to get them to talk practically. I ask, "What if the soldiers come and put you in a van and take you out of here? Has anyone been here to talk to you? To explain things? Tell you your options?" They shake their heads. "But we get great offers in the mail. 'Build your dream house in Manara [which is on the Lebanese border] with a free *dunam* of land!'" Roz laughs. "We are not consciously prepared to do anything to help the Disengagement," Paul says. "But if they come to take us, if they cart me away, I'm not going to fight anyone. I'll go." Roz explains that each family has paid in NIS 1,000 (about $300) to a group of 100 lawyers who are working mostly pro-bono to stop the Disengagement through the courts. "We're not doing anything. They are doing it all." Although the Schneids are reluctant to talk about money, the general sentiment of settlers is that the compensation the government is offering will impoverish most of them. For example, it will pay for the loss of their hothouses, but not for their produce or business revenues.

Paul and Roz are set to accompany us to the army checkpoint that marks the entrance to Gush Katif. As we drive, we pass the beautiful synagogue, and the dorms of the yeshiva students, and the just-completed community center, empty of furniture because there is no funding, nor is there likely to be. We pass the group of 27 homes put up by Ariel Sharon when he was Minister of Housing. He did it in one night, just before the signing of the Oslo Accords, Roz tells me. We pass the beautiful wooden house donated by the community to serve as a rest and recreation area for soldiers protecting the community, a place where they can take a can of coke from the fridge or have some coffee and cake, supplied daily by the community's grateful families. It is named in the memory of Tali Hatuel and her four girls.

I hold my breath as we take the road out. It is an ugly place, Gaza. The fields and trees which once lined the sides of the roads have been uprooted since they were used for cover by snipers targeting settlers. The houses near the road have been bulldozed, following their use in terrorist attacks. The place is full of army camps, watchtowers, army vehicles, and soldiers. And still, I don't feel safe.

If the Disengagement takes place, nothing will mark the spot where all these things took place. The sand will blow, covering the spot where all the blood was spilled; and politics will continue, the Arab-Israeli conflict entering a new stage, with more demands and counter-demands, more terrorist attacks and more efforts to prevent them that will no doubt involve the continued death of innocents.

As we stop at the checkpoint before leaving, I embrace Roz and wish her well. "Whatever happens, I'm not worried about myself," she tells me. "We'll get along. We'll get a pension. We'll rent a house. We'll manage. It's not me I'm worried about. I'm worried about the Jewish people. I'm worried about the future of this country."

In the car on the way home, I think about the way the Schneids have lived their lives, their pioneering spirit, their beautiful family, their sons in the army, their daughter the doctor. I wonder if in August, Paul, weak from chemo, will be manhandled by Israeli soldiers and put on a truck together with Roz. I wonder if their house will be bulldozed with all the family photos, if their hot-houses will be destroyed with the crops still in them; if the synagogue which lost its Rabbi will be blown up by Israeli troops, if the bodies of terror victims who lived and died and were buried in Gaza will be disinterred and transferred too. And suddenly, I, too, am worried about the future of my country.

130,000 in Human Chain from Gush Katif to Jerusalem

By Tovah Lazaroff and Matthew Gutman

This article appeared in The Jerusalem Post, July 26, 2004.

"Don't evacuate us," wrote six-year-old Yael Better in a note that she stuck in a crevice in the Western Wall.

She was the last participant in a human protest chain anchored by her grandfather, Yitzchak Shamir, one of the founders of Kfar Darom, who lost an arm and a leg fighting for the Gaza Strip settlement during the War of Independence in 1948.

The chain, the first of its kind in Israel and the third longest in history, stretched over a span of 90 kilometers (55 miles) to Jerusalem. Police said that an estimated 130,000 people linked hands Sunday evening to protest the Disengagement Plan.

The two-hour event ended at 7 p.m., with the singing of the national anthem "Hatikva" and the blowing of three large horns, with blasts that sounded like shofars, at the Western Wall. While its organizers stressed that the human chain was "a chain linking the people of Israel," the string of humanity also served as a political bludgeon.

"This is the spearhead of the settlements passive resistance campaign," said Avner Avraham, who trekked up from Eilat to Kibbutz Yad Mordechai with his six young children to protest the evacuation. "This is about love, but it is also about showing Sharon that physically he will not be able to uproot Jews from their homes."

Avraham wore a T-shirt with large block letters that spelled out the words "BAD JOKE." He was convinced that that is how the majority of Israelis feel about the evacuation.

Certainly that is how Better's grandfather Shamir, Avram Dimant, and their comrades – all of them nearing their ninth decade – feel.

They had virtually chained themselves to the original incarnation of the embattled settlement during Israel's 1948 War of Independence. "We refused to leave, even though we survived on half a cup of water and a cube of chocolate a day for weeks," said Dimant, then-commander of the outpost.

"That is why we cannot allow another pullback from any piece of land in the middle of a war," said Shamir, who served as the first link in the chain just outside the Erez Checkpoint, north of the Gaza Strip.

Purchased by Jews in 1946, Kfar Darom earned fame as a beacon of Israeli self-sacrifice and bravery in the face of an unrelenting Egyptian onslaught. Eventually, Israel's founding father, David Ben-Gurion, personally ordered its members to abandon the settlement.

The chain drew Israelis and visitors from around the world, including non-Jews. Current events mingled with Biblical history. Many demonstrators hailed from religious backgrounds and it was their faith, they said, which compelled them to believe that it was their duty to prevent the evacuation.

The event was specifically scheduled for the day before Tisha B'Av, a day of mourning for the destruction of the First and Second Temples, in order to underscore what many settlers consider the catastrophic potential of the Disengagement Plan.

In Jerusalem, at the top of Jaffa Road, a group of 53 Independent Baptists from the United States held hands and sang, "Don't give away Gush Katif, Sharon."

One of their organizers, Pastor Bob Ross from Oklahoma, said, "We believe, as Zionist Christians that Jehovah God clearly promises his blessings on those who bless Israel. We want to be a blessing to Israel," all of it, including the Gaza Strip. Among the participants was Dan Davidovitch, whose 30-year-old daughter Ahuva Amergi of Gush Katif was killed in a terrorist attack in February 2002. The son of a Holocaust survivor, he sat by Jerusalem's Central Bus Station with a large photograph of Ahuva stuck on the baby carriage of a new granddaughter, named for Ahuva.

Ahuva herself was named for one of his father's seven children, who were killed in the Holocaust. "My father lost 33 people," said Davidovitch. He recalled how Justice Minister Yosef Lapid said that the picture of an old Palestinian woman sifting through the rubble of her destroyed home in Rafiach following an IDF attack reminded him of the Holocaust.

"I want to tell Lapid that talk of disengagement reminds me of stories my father told me about forcing Jews to leave their homes during the Holocaust," said Davidovitch. "We came to show the world that no force will take Jews away from their land."

In a parade-like atmosphere, supporters of Gush Katif lined the roads, brandished signs at drivers, waved and sang.

Knesset Speaker and Likud MK Reuven Rivlin and Likud Minister Natan Sharansky were among the 20 politicians, including MKs from the National Union and the National Religious Party, who participated in the event.

Police mobilized thousands of officers, reinforced by more than 1,000 private security guards, to patrol the route, deal with snarled traffic, and prevent any attempt to create a disturbance. Motorists were advised to take alternate routes. Nearly 900 buses were rented to bring people to various points along the route, said one of the organizers, Zevulun Halfon.

The coordination of the settlement organizers was precise. Hundreds of volunteers herded children off the curbs and ensured that the right people arrived at the right places at the right time. Like good soldiers, parents and toddlers moved to fill gaps in the human chain. Organizers on foot and in jeeps shuttled up and down the line ensuring order.

While Gush Katif spokeswoman Rachel Saperstein warned that provocateurs might try to stir things up, the demonstration ended peacefully. There were no reports of incitement against Sharon. In fact, the chain's ending seemed anti-climactic along the roads near Gaza. Demonstrators all along the route finished singing "Hatikva" and, not knowing what to do, began strolling toward waiting buses and hitching rides.

Thousands of youths and adults turned toward Jerusalem for their evening prayers just after the completion of the national anthem. During downtimes, many read psalms by the roadside.

In Jerusalem, veteran Yitzchak Shamir's daughter, Tamar Better, held her daughter after the chain disbanded and said, "This is a very emotional moment. Our family is the story of the chain, and we hope it will continue."

Her husband, Mordechai Better, added, "I don't know if it will have any influence. But we at least want to show the government that this can't be given up easily. There are three generations here."

Photo provided by Debbie Rosen
The Human Chain

The Prayer of the Sixty Thousand
By Rabbi Yosef Elnekaveh

August 10, 2005

Over the past year, mass prayer services have been held in Jerusalem, Gush Katif, and at holy gravesites. Each one appealed to a certain crowd in terms of the types of prayers that were said. These prayers and supplications were recited with great emotion and many tears, reminiscent of the Ten Days of Repentance. Jews stood together, deeply moved, shedding tears, united in their prayer that the expulsion decree would be rescinded. Yet the most unique of all these rallies has to be yesterday's ceremony at the Western Wall. Jews from all backgrounds, communities, and sectors of the population, including national religious, ultra orthodox, and other parts of the spectrum, united in their tears, supplications, and heartfelt entreaties to the One Above. There was a certain feeling of historical significance in this prayer, hopefully it would be accepted and annul the decree [of Disengagement].

In the words of the Prophet, "Like the flocks of Jerusalem in their festive seasons, so will be the destroyed cities." This is how I felt yesterday, as if I were following in the spirit of this prophecy. As I walked through the alleyways of Jerusalem, I could see the endless crowd. Every street was packed. The organizers told us that from Agron Street to the City of David, the area was so crowded that there was no room to move. I personally witnessed the throngs of people wanting to show their moral support for the residents of Gush Katif and give us their heartfelt blessings.

This rally was truly unique, both in terms of quantity and quality. Mystics, Chabad Rabbis, and leaders of the "Litvish" community all stood together. Our tradition states that even if the Jewish people were, God forbid, to serve idols, if we were united, no other nation or race could conquer us. I really believe that since the Second Temple era, there has never been such a united gathering at the Western Wall. Everyone else had the same feeling, too. For a brief moment, I imagined how Jerusalem must have looked during the festive seasons, such as *on the eve of Passover*, when the entire nation gathered to offer the Passical sacrifice.

Incidentally, I am sure that when the Third Temple descends from the Heavens, or, according to other opinions, is constructed by man, suitable solutions to the problems of traffic, parking, and the transportation of sheep will be found. Former Prime Minister Ehud Barak actually thought of one of these solutions. When he wanted to hand over parts of Jerusalem to the Arabs, as well as the rights to the Temple Mount, Barak looked into the possibility of building bridges that would create more access options to the Temple Mount. If this idea was good enough for the Arabs at this time, it would surely also be possible to adopt it during Temple times.

Similar to other such gatherings, the shofar was blown, along with trumpets. With each blast, we felt subdued and in awe, rather like during the High Holy Days. In a spirit of glory, we could feel a sense of self-nullification, and we wished that we could see the miracle right away. Sometimes, when we speak about the Messiah, it almost feels fanciful. Yet yesterday we all saw him between the cracks of the Western Wall. It was so hard to move and we all stood squashed together. I suddenly looked up toward the Wall and saw some pure white doves between the cracks of its stones, lamenting the sorrow of Israel, the pain of the Divine Spirit.

At the same time that the Jewish masses were gathered in Jerusalem, a special, moving prayer ceremony for children took place here in Gush Katif. It is a known fact that the prayers of Jewish children can storm the gates of Heaven. And while this is said of all Jewish children, it is particularly applicable to the children of Gush Katif. These children are so unique in their uncompromising love for the land of Israel. I do not think I would be wrong in saying that the main inspiration in every home in Gush Katif and the leading force that motivates the adult population at every such prayer assembly or gathering come from the children and youth.

They possess such purity and they will tell you that the Expulsion won't happen. They are not prepared to consider even the remotest possibility that it will. In many families, the children and young people argue with their parents over this issue. The children exude such a spirit of faith and they are the ones who have ignited the orange flame that burns in all of our hearts.

This week, I heard a very apt expression from one young man that I have since adopted for myself. He said, "There is nothing more blue and white than orange." This is what he said, and if you stop to think about it, it is so true. For us, blue and white represents the sanctity of the Jewish state. Fifty-seven years since the establishment of the state, the time has come to introduce within the blue and white something that has come from the children. It is something that nourishes and nurtures a certain faith within that beautiful framework.

When we arrived at the Western Wall, we burst into song: "Have mercy with Your loving-kindness upon your people, our Rock, upon Zion, the Sanctuary of Your glory, the ruin of the House of our Glory. May the son of David, Your servant, come to redeem us." This is the favorite song of the former Sephardi Chief Rabbi, Rabbi Mordechai Eliyahu. At every rally – at the Western Wall, the Cave of Rabbi Shimon Bar Yochai, the olive spring of Rabbi Yehudah Berabi Illai, at the tomb of the Baba Sali in Netivot, at the Mount of Olives, at the gravesite of the Orach Chaim, and on Har Hamenuchot at the gravesite of the Chida, Rabbi Eliyahu always asks Roni Ben David to sing this song.

Needless to say, this song was composed by the famous Chief Rabbi of Gaza, Rabbi Yisrael Najara, who first lived in Tzefat, the glorious city of the famous Arizal. From there he moved to Gaza, where he remained for the rest of his life. After his death, his descendants continued to serve as the Chief Rabbis of Gaza City.

As we passed through the Dung Gate the verse, "Even if I return in darkness, God will light my way," sprang to mind. We are all "believers, the children of believers," and we are well aware of the sharp sword hanging over our heads. But we must never give up, because even though the intellect is extremely important and we can use our powers of understanding to fulfill our goals, there are things that go way beyond the intellect. Such things are defined as faith. For while the intellect is limited and finite, faith has no limits. In some ways, faith is like a dream. With faith you could uproot two huge mountains and grind them into dust. Through it, you can connect the land and the sea. That is the definition of true, basic, fundamental faith. Its power is so strong and it is at the spiritual foundation of the Jewish people.

As I stood watching the flow of people, I remarked that if next Monday, 10 Menachem Av, a similarly huge crowd would flock to the Kissufim Crossing, we would be sure to see the Messiah face to face.

One woman replied that we had already witnessed so many miracles. "You residents of Gush Katif live with miracles," she said. But one of the greatest miracles of all had to be this crowd of hundreds of thousands of Jews in Jerusalem, who all stood together. Black *kippot* mingled with knitted and orange *kippot*, and headscarves, hats, and wigs were seen throughout the crowd, and all of these different people were united in prayer, language, faith, and hope. And together we said, "Many waters could not quench this love."

From the Diary of a Former Gaza Resident

By Dr. Pesach Aceman

August 15, 2005

I must write today, as I do not know what will be tomorrow. Whether there will be a phone line or electricity, or what?

Last night, there were two loud explosions very close to our house. Kassam rockets exploding. Sent by our Arab neighbors, who by the way, 'agreed' to not fire. Nevertheless it seems that our army is too busy with Expulsion to respond, as usual these past few weeks. Didn't disturb the basketball players though.

It is such a topsy-turvy world, emotionally-wise. Today, the press in all its forms came to our gate, as they did to several of the communities in Gush Katif. The gate was closed (a large electric gate) immediately as there is disgust for the sharks that have invaded the waters where blood is being spilled. At our settlement the police and army arrive, but to no avail. They were not allowed in, and in many communities they 'retreated' for now so as to avoid any confrontation. People are in pain. More and more are staying to what we can say will be the end (or beginning) despite having packed up. It is such an emotionally painful experience that most want to stay with their neighbors/friends of over a quarter of a century to share what may be these last moments.

Certainly that was the feeling on Sunday during the special prayer services for the fast day (Tisha B'Av, which commemorates the loss of the First and Second Temples, the expulsion from Spain, and the first day of the Warsaw Ghetto uprising, among others). The service was so uplifting, and the shared pain of over 500 people (which caused us to move outside of the synagogue for lack of room) was beyond description.

The Spirits are Good

I, as a physician, have joined the medical team that will be here after the clinics are closed. I went to Neve Dekalim, the largest community in Gush Katif with over 600 families, to see if there was something I could do to help the ob/gyn doctor who comes once a week. The gate was closed; on one side stood a row of police and soldiers, on the other side many people preventing these "guardians" of the State from entering. It also prevented any traffic in or out, as well as the moving vans from entering to collect those who packed up their belongings, some of which have been hired by the army to provoke more psychological warfare and inflame hostilities. So I walked to the clinic.

I then went to check on my daughter at the gate to our community and pass out some cold water. It is over 33 degrees Celsius! It was not confrontational but ended with the army withdrawing. But for how long? A few hours, a day, or maybe, with G-d's help, forever?

A friend invited me for coffee and we talked. They also are not packing up anything. So we talked and then he showed me what he had written yesterday. A painful, yet very emotional account of our prayer service and his doubts and his not knowing as well what lies ahead.

What will the next hour, next day hold?

We need to replenish some food supplies for now.

Then today again the alarm goes out to all that the soldiers have returned. Again, with singing and a throng of people, no soldier enters and they leave.

Now it has become a cycle that will probably repeat itself over and over during the next 24 hours. It has been reported that our eviction/expulsion will be postponed to another day. Everyone, except for a minority, does not want any violence and will do their utmost to continue demonstrating to delay/prevent the eviction notices from being served on the residents of the various communities.

Some see this as a fight to the end and liken this to the Holocaust. But we are not going to death camps to be annihilated. There is no comparison! Those that see this as a fight to the end liken it to the uprising in the Warsaw Ghetto. There, it was a fight to the end knowing that without a miracle, there was no victory but the dignity of fighting to the last man with all their strength. They knew where the next stop was! I do not feel we are in the same boat at all. We must do all in our power to hold back and to try to invoke changes of heart in the very soldiers that are at the gates. Will this be enough? Will there be resorting to violence to demonstrate that what is felt by all here in Gush Katif is wrong?

We have had electricity outages, garbage piling up as the garbage collection is stopped, medical services officially stop today, but we are organized to provide round the clock service and just about everything is covered by volunteers. The terror continues, and so does the basketball.

I was moved to tears by a very simple thing today. When I walked the dogs, the grass around part of the yishuv was wet, and at another house the grass was being watered.

Small signs of great faith and hope.

Diaries of the Last Days of Gush Katif
By Toby Klein Greenwald

This article originally appeared in aish.com, a leading Judaism website.

Tuesday, August 9, 2005

My husband, Yaakov, and I get up early and drive down to Atzmona to baby-sit our granddaughters. Our daughter, Naama, is part of a Gush Katif women's theater group and today is their last performance – at a conference in Bar Ilan University. Her husband, Avner, a career officer and captain in the IDF, will be home late. She takes her three-month-old son, Oz Naftali, with her, as she is still nursing him.

I think how appropriate his name Naftali is – for it is after my father, who died this year, who loved to travel. Oz Naftali has also been all over Israel with his mother's theater group. They perform an original play that expresses their doubts, their fears, and their faith in these troubled times.

The community of Atzmona looks like it does every other day. There are no moving containers, no unusual activity. No one in Atzmona is packing. This is a community with no televisions and no secular newspapers. Many of the residents are teachers in yeshivot and schools. The others are farmers who are a part of Atzmona's successful agricultural community. Their farming industry has paid off well, but they live modestly, with mid-size homes surrounded by lawns and flowers. But some of the homes, including our daughter's, have black indentations in the outside walls – from the shrapnel of mortars that have fallen here. One fell 20 feet from our daughter's home, among the blooming yellow alemandra plants.

We drive with our granddaughters, Tehila and Shirel, to Neve Dekalim, seven minutes away. Our plan was to take them to the petting zoo, but there is a sign that it is closed, some people say, because of the nine days leading up to Tisha B'Av, when one doesn't partake of entertainment. But as a former camp director, I know that zoos are among the few activities allowed, and I suspect it is closed because some of the animals have already been transferred to other zoos. My suspicions are confirmed by a friend who lives in Neve Dekalim, who tells me how they gently tied orange ribbons around the donkeys' ears before they sent them off to Kibbutz Saad, so everyone would know they were from Gush Katif.

The lawns and shopping center are full of vibrant young people, reading, playing basketball, eating, and just talking. It is a blazingly hot day. The local ice cream and coffee shop, well air-conditioned, is brimming with soldiers, local residents, and visiting journalists with laptops. We stop in at the local medical center to visit the girls' other grandmother, Ruti Cohen, whose sister and brother-in-law were shot dead three weeks ago by a Palestinian policeman on Tzir Kissufim, the main road leading in and out of Gush Katif. This is Ruti's first day back at work. As she holds Shirel on her lap, we watch a dentist wheeling the contents of his clinic out of the center. A doctor and several psychologists, who have come from Jerusalem and Beit Shemesh to volunteer their time, look in and say hello. Magazines about the Land of Israel are on the tables in the waiting area, along with toys and dolls.

We continue to a large and beautiful playground. While my granddaughters climb and slide, I lie on my back, look up at the sky, and wonder what God wants from us. I look at the sun and the sea, and at the immense beauty that has been created here, from out of the sand dunes.

Later that day, when it is cool enough to go outside, I play with Tehila and Shirel and their friends. We sit on their grass and catch imaginary fish, make imaginary honey, prepare imaginary challot for Shabbat. But when I suggest that we (pretend to) pick oranges and make orange juice, they run to a bush with red flowers, pick some branches, pull off some of the red flowers, pretend they are oranges, and suck the nectar. They tell me this is a trick they have learned on their way to pre-school – to suck the nectar from the red flowers.

Later, the farmers from Atzmona drop off a large sack of potatoes in front of every home – a gift. The girls make a game of pulling the potatoes out of the sack, one by one, and lining them up in front of the kitchen door. This keeps them busy for about 30 minutes. Such are the activities of children growing up among farmers, with no TV.

Naama, Oz Naftali, and Avner come home together. Yaakov and I have already fed and bathed the girls. I have made Tehila five pigtails, as she asked, and a little braid for Shirel. They hide under the sheets and jump out at their father. I take Oz Naftali out for a long walk to help him quiet down, and stop to visit a friend who is the sister of the *Rebbetzin* of Atzmona.

Chaya is a parenting adviser, and she tells me how she is trying to explain to the women that it is "okay" to put some cherished objects into a backpack at least, even if they don't want to pack, to save the children's special collections and other items, in case they are lost when the soldiers come to pack.

I fall asleep broken-hearted.

Wednesday, August 10

I get up before the others and decide to drive to every single community in Gush Katif that I haven't visited yet. As I make my way from one to the other, I see that some look like any other day, and a few, like Pe'at Sadeh, have moving containers in front of the homes, or the homes have already been left and there is orange graffiti on them – "anti-Disengagement" or "I love you Gush Katif." I see a horse in one of the yards, whose owners have not yet left.

I drive along the seashore to Rafiach Yam, where I know the Attiya family. I knock on their door to say hello. There is no answer, but a reserve officer named Dan tells me that they must be sleeping. There are boxes in front of the house. Dan invites me around the corner to the soldiers' quarters, where he has the Attiyas' cell phone number. While I wait for it, I see that this makeshift soldiers' quarters has religious books and pamphlets lying around. Dan is from a moshav in the Negev and he says, "It is hard, it is hard to be here now."

I continue to Bedolach, Gan-Or, Gadid. As I enter each community, I nod and say hello to the soldier on guard. As I leave, I stop the car and salute in the direction of the settlement. I choose to salute because they are like soldiers, who have been sent here by Israeli governments. I, too, was sent to Efrat in Gush Etzion by the Israeli government. I salute them as one soldier to another.

I reach Shirat Hayam and Kfar Yam, where hundreds of families and young people have created tent cities. I see a young neighbor from Efrat, Rivka Bedein, who is studying medical clowning and has come to entertain the children.

I drive back to my daughter's home and we get ready to leave. At noon, we will be attending a brit milah in Ganei Tal. A new grandson has been born to other in-laws who live there, the Asis family. I whisper to Naama as I hug her, "I am so proud of you." She, Israeli that she is, replies, "Stop, Ima, you're embarrassing me." As I leave Naama's home for what I fear is the last time, I turn around and exit backwards, like in a synagogue. This, I think to myself, is like the Temple in Jerusalem. I kiss the mezuzah as I step out. I am leaving a sanctuary of faith and love.

Shirel, who just ran through someone's sprinkler and got wet (yes, they are still watering the lawn one week before the expulsion), has taken off all her clothes. She is only three years old and I laugh as she runs, naked, all the way to our car, enjoying her freedom and the fact that her mother, unlike me, isn't thrilled about her lack of attire.

We drive to Ganei Tal and see a crowd that is not only friends and family, but supporters who have used the excuse of a brit milah to enter the Gush. The baby's grandfather tells us that he has made five trips that day back and forth to Ashkelon, to which he has transferred his greenhouses of geraniums and spices. Everyone, even those of great faith, recognize that it may be the last brit milah in Gush Katif, and the atmosphere is heavily mixed with joy and sorrow. The lawns surrounding the synagogue are filled with well-wishers, the tables laden with cold drinks and watermelon slices. The child is named Amichai – "my nation lives."

During the festive lunch (at tables decorated with orange ribbons and napkins), the Rabbi of the community, Gabi Kadosh, the baby's other grandfather, says, "I invite you all to join us here for Amichai's *Shabbat chatan* (the Shabbat before a wedding)!" One of the caterer's workers rolls his eyes in disbelief. But I say to the people at my table, "Amichai's father married young, at 19. And I remember how the children of Gush Etzion returned to their homes after the Six Day War in 1967, 19 years after they were driven out in 1948 when Gush Etzion fell to the Jordanians. These children, too, will return one day."

I finish my little speech of hope and Chanan Porat enters the hall to wish the family mazal tov. Chanan was the leader of the Gush Etzion children who returned in 1967, and I declare it to be an omen that my prophecy was true, and that the children of Gush Katif will return, one day, to this strip of land.

Friday, August 12

We leave for a day and are now returning for *Shabbat Chazon*, the Shabbat before Tisha B'Av, the Shabbat during which we read *Parashat Devarim*, which tells how the Land of Israel was given to us. We spend Shabbat in Ganei Tal. Naama is also there with her family, as is another daughter, Noa, also married to a boy who grew up in Ganei Tal; they have decided to spend this Shabbat with his parents as well. Our daughter, Ephrat, 22, has been in Gush Katif for a week already and Matanya, 15, comes in with us. We have "passes" to be in Gush Katif till midnight Saturday night. I express the desire to leave, therefore, after midnight – my tiny protest against the government. Ephrat and Matanya say they will be staying on. As it turns out, there is shooting on the Kissufim Route Saturday night and we delay our leaving till the next day.

Friday night, the air conditioning in the synagogue shuts off as prayers are about to begin. There are several hundred visitors in this community of about 70 families, and the hundreds move outside to pray, in a plaza surrounded by trees, where wedding feasts are usually held. Naama and Avner, whose *chuppah* took place on the grass overlooking the seashore, held their wedding feast here as well. I cannot believe that after this week they will not be able to return to the site of their *chuppah*, to the site of their wedding. The prayers are so powerful, so deeply wrenching, that I feel we are standing on the eve of Yom Kippur. I half expect, after the reciting of *Shema Yisrael*, to hear the congregation add the next line, *"Baruch shem kavod"* aloud, like on the eve of Kol Nidre, not quietly, like the rest of the year.

The next morning, there are tears in shul. Nobody can escape the thought that this is probably the last Shabbat in Ganei Tal, though most people still speak with a tone of hope, praying for a miracle. The Rabbi speaks from the pulpit about the power of miracles and how God can do anything, but his final words are, "In the coming days, let us feel also a sense of joy, and give thanks for all the good we have received."

The man to close the ark after the returning of the Torah is Zalman Deutsch of Alon Shvut, the architect who built this shul more than 20 years ago. He pulls the curtain closed and leans forward to kiss it gently. During the repeat of the Musaf Amidah prayer, the *kohanim* [priests] ascend the steps at the front, turn, and bless the congregation. I have a son-in-law up there and I watch him and his brother and father as they face the Ark, after the blessing. The *kohanim* remain up there for longer than usual, unable to part, knowing this may have been the last time they bless their friends and neighbors.

A grand *Kiddush* follows, the cakes and kugels provided by supporters throughout Israel who have sent their love and food to Gush Katif. A man announces that the *Kiddush* next Shabbat will be on the lawn of one of the residents. People cheer, knowing that there may not be another Shabbat here in Ganei Tal. There are tears and laughter throughout the day.

There are two concepts that keep guiding me and that I think we have to keep in our minds. One is our own *hishtadlut*, doing whatever we can to avert the decree of expulsion. The other is that God has His plan.

These two concepts are not contradictory. The Holy One can do anything.

Saturday night, Tisha B'Av begins and we listen to the reading of *Lamentations*, which describes the destruction of both Holy Temples. The symbolism is overwhelming. Again, the plaza is filled with young people and old, mothers under trees with babies, like in days of old. Everyone is struck by the words in

Chapter 5: "Our inheritance has been turned over to strangers, our homes to aliens."

Sunday, August 14

Let no one tell you that the people who are packing up their belongings are leaving "willingly," as the press is trying to paint it. We know one family that was packing, even appropriately, on Tisha B'Av, as a sign of the destruction of the Temple. They planned to leave at the last minute, but decided they did not want to leave even a light bulb for the Palestinians to loot. The father of the home, alluding to a biblical verse, said, "They have murdered and they will also inherit?" Ruti Cohen, on the other hand, said to me, "I will walk out of here with only two Shabbat candlesticks and a photograph [of Rachel and Dov]."

We do not know the ways of God. But the togetherness and sanctification of God's name over the last year must count for something. One area in which we've already witnessed the result of this *Kiddush Hashem* is in the changed tone of many of the TV reporters.

Many reporters join the hundreds of residents at the Gush Katif cemetery, where 48 people – many of them victims of terror – are buried and will have to be exhumed. They stand under the blazing sun and pray, and sing songs pleading for salvation.

Monday, August 15

My husband and I have left Gush Katif, but have stayed in close contact with our children and other relatives there. The people of Ganei Tal, until then considered a suburban, boomer-aged community that would go quietly, block the entrance to the moshav. The army actually has to turn around and decides to give the expulsion notices later. An officer from the Golani brigade, now a civilian and staying in Morag, meets his former commander who has come to give expulsion notices. He bursts into tears and asks, "How can you do this? Our enemy is over there (pointing to Khan Yunis). We fought shoulder to shoulder. They have been killing us. How can you throw us out? We love you!" The senior officer embraces him and tries to hold back his own tears.

In Netzarim, a strongly religious settlement, it is business as usual. People continue to build several new houses and to plant trees. There is a joke going around that, when the miracle happens and a feast of thanksgiving takes place, the people from Netzarim won't understand what it's all about because they never acknowledged the Disengagement to begin with.

A woman from Ganei Tal is asked by a reporter, "What will you do when soldiers enter your house and tell you that you have to leave?" "I will give them a history lesson," she answers.

The youth are everywhere, especially in Neve Dekalim. The army cannot control them. They did not know what awaited them. Even the youth from the northern settlements of Gaza, like Elei Sinai, mostly secular, from which some residents have left, have barricaded themselves in and refuse to go.

A professor of psychology from Ben Gurion University is interviewed by Israel TV. She says that the previous week she examined both adults and youth in Gush Katif. Her comment on the youth: "They care about the country. They care about the army. They care about democracy. And there is one way is which they are especially different from the secular youth we usually see: they don't care about money."

Tuesday, August 16

Avi Farhan is interviewed on the radio. When Israel gave the Sinai Peninsula to Egypt in 1983, he was uprooted from Yamit and walked all the way to Jerusalem. Now he is about to be expelled from Elei Sinai. Farhan says, "I cannot transplant a tree twice – once when I move into temporary housing and then again when we move into another permanent house. Any agronomist will tell you that when a tree is uprooted twice, it will die. Except for the olive tree. It can survive a second uprooting. I hope that my children will be like the olive tree."

The day has passed with clashes in Neve Dekalim and elsewhere. There is much discussion on the news about the "illegals" – mostly, but not exclusively, teenagers who have managed to sneak into Gush Katif. They number in the thousands. A few of them get out of hand and burn or puncture tires. Some people pack, others live as usual. There are complaints from communities that have been split up, and even some of those who have gone willingly – particularly from the northern settlements – have had a rude awakening by the shoddy, tiny caravans to which they were sent.

I speak to Ruti and to Naama in the course of the day. Naama is busy, taking the girls from activity to activity. Volunteers have poured into all the settlements to help with the children.

By nightfall, the remaining people in Gush Katif – and it is still the majority, even though they have been told they will lose one third of their compensation – await with trembling the knock on the door. For on Wednesday morning, the real expulsion will begin.

A Diary With No Title
By Chaim Gibber

August 14, 2005 (9 Av, 5765)

As I am not sure who this is meant for, I will leave the title empty for the time being. I, for one, don't fully understand what's happening or, for that matter, even why. What we do know is that they [whoever they might be] are trying to destroy our beautiful community with its true Torah values and serene way of life. The pressures that have been brought to bear on us in the last months have caused some of the moshav to fold and give up the fight. They will be leaving by the 17th of August, while the rest of us under the leadership of our Rav, will be remaining until we are physically evicted. I ask you not necessarily to accept our decision, but on the other hand, as you are not in our shoes, please don't judge us either.

I had a very different perspective on the "when to pack" issue than my children did, and so at first I insisted that the boys come home from yeshiva to pack at least that part of the house that had sentimental value. Although totally against it on principle, they came home to pack in a most professional fashion (without a smile).

As the time went on, and the deadline got closer, and nerves started to fray at the edges, we convened as a family to draw certain guidelines. As a result, we decided not to pack any more and to leave the pictures still hanging on the walls, at least until after Tisha B'Av. And so it was. Since that decision, I, for one, am breathing a little easier, and the top level of frayed nerves has come down a peg or two. Our main objective as of now is to maintain our family's health both physically and mentally, and we are now even more united as a family, as well as stronger as a community.

I spent all day Thursday preparing to be absent from work for as long as it may take. I prepared a schedule of manure removal, as well as a feed order and any other delivery for the month. I programmed the computer with all the ongoing changes through the end of the month, checked the generator and all the emergency equipment, and then finally left for home, but not before going over every aspect of the operation with the German engineer who installed the entire project. I felt that I left everything in good hands and was free to concentrate on the family problems. That idea was shattered already on Friday when I got a frantic call that no one was able to start the egg collectors and it was just the beginning of the weekend. I stayed on the phone for about half an hour and fortunately we were able to get things back on line.

Friday morning we loaded the empty gas bottles on my car as was agreed by the family. David and I proceeded to take the cars out of the moshav before the 15th, as no one had answers as to how they might get out after that date. I wanted to take the computer with me, but the boys refused to let me remove anything from the house. Gathering strength from their resolve, I left with a good feeling that I was doing the right thing.

Shabbat came in with a bang. I guess you will need some background to understand that last statement. The government has tried to close off this area and not allow in non-residents, in order to carry out the eviction with as little resistance as possible. However, as in Egypt of old, the harder the government fought, the more persevering the supporters got. And so with the efforts of people like our Aryeh, who led families in through fields at night and other unconventional activities, by that Friday afternoon if you were lucky, you could still find a tree to set up your tent and call it your deluxe accommodations.

August 14, 2005 (9 Av, 5765) – Later in the Day

We had families who came in to shower, and others that accepted our invitation to sleep in a bed as well. Joyce was just lighting candles when all the electricity in the house went out. I quickly determined that one of the air conditioners in the living room was the cause, shut it off, and everything else stayed on. When I got to shul, I found that the shul was dark and everyone was on the lawn, en masse, *davening* [praying] together. The *davening* was particularly long, but very moving. As we were only the six of us around the table Friday night, we ate in the kitchen, where the air conditioning was still working.

On Shabbat morning, with several air conditioners on the fritz, the shul filled to three times its capacity, and the summer heat at its best, you can imagine what davening was like. The Rav gave a very moving sermon, and the walls shook from the vigor of the davening and the singing went on and on. At the end of davening, when one of the founding members of the moshav got up and spoke about his feelings and ended off with the singing of *Machnisei Rachamim*, there wasn't a dry eye in the place. One had to be there to appreciate the impact of the moment. As hot as it was, no one was rushing home. A *Kiddush* was sponsored by the non-members to cheer up the members; they even served and cleaned up. For lunch, we had company and were now 13 around the table, so we moved out to under the tree. Zalman Deutsch, the architect of our shul, together with our neighbors, joined us for the day. After lunch there was an *Oneg Shabbat* at which time the Rav asked everyone to stay together as a group, but anyone leaving before the group should be sure to stop in so he could kiss them goodbye. (By the way, except for two families who are moving away, the difference between those leaving now or later is only a matter of days.)

As the sun started setting it was obvious to all that this would be a Tisha B'Av to be remembered. The *megillah* [*Lamentations*] was read outside and broadcast over the loudspeakers. With close to five hundred people present, there were hardly enough *kinot* [liturgical poems of mourning traditionally recited on Tisha B'Av] to share. The *kinot* were read aloud for all to hear. (Can you imagine such a scene in Monticello?) A very moving experience.

Emotionally drained, we went to sleep early, just to be awakened by a power outage about 2:30 a.m. We thought the worst – the army is cutting us off ahead of schedule to force us out. Many other thoughts crossed my mind in those few hours. We hadn't yet prepared a water supply. Or checked the freezers. It was a false alarm, but a good practice for what's in store for us.

Davening this morning was also emotional, but not quite the impact of last night. The day took off soon after, with a meeting of all the families who were staying to the end to set up committees to arrange food, water, communication, youth activities, and the basic needs of the group. Our David is on the board of five in charge of the entire operation. So far he has volunteered to organize the youth and control the collection of garbage. That meeting ended at about 11:30. At 12:00 we left for the cemetery, where thousands showed up to pay last respects to the many friends and children buried there. There were the sounds of shofars and singing, part of davening from Yom Kippur and *selichot* [prayers for forgiveness], asking Hashem to have mercy on us. Although everyone was fasting and the sun was hot, still no one wanted to leave. After over two hours, feeling emotionally drained, we returned home to rest. Hadar, who was out learning until three in the morning, had to be awakened to finish a film she was preparing for the BBC, then went back to sleep. Joyce went up to sleep, and the boys fell asleep on the couch. I spent most of the day at the computer on this letter. I was called out about five o'clock to fix the electric gate of the moshav in an attempt to keep out press and other unwanted individuals.

Section Two:

Expulsion and Desecration

The Walls That Had the Last Word
Photos Provided by Debbie Rosen

In every house in Gush Katif, there was a son or a daughter who insisted on writing his/her memories on the walls of his/her home. Each one is written from the heart:

GOD IS WITH US! GUSH KATIF!
The People of Israel

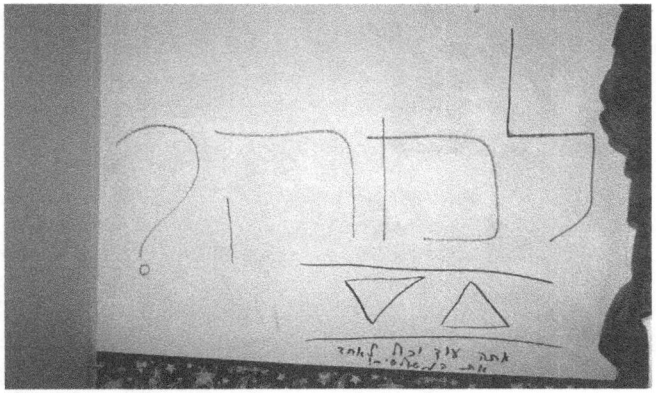

WHY?
[It's not too late] You can still unify the 'triangles'
[to make a unified symbol of the Star of David]

Dear Soldier!

Hello, My name is Netta Rosen and I [have] lived here, in this room since I was born, 17.5 years [ago]. I just wanted to tell you that when you come to destroy my room, and my whole house, that I hope you feel happy with yourself, or at least OK. For you lent a hand to this sin of eviction of innocent Jews from their house, and destroyed whole lives for nothing and in exchange of nothing. Because in another 10 years, when the terrible results of this expulsion will be clear to all, and all the people will suffer from it — yes, you as well and the family you will have — what will you say? What will you tell yourself, that you carried out your orders?? What will you tell your children, that because you evicted Jews from their house 10 years ago, they can't go to the mall??

Understand, we love you soldiers very much, and we love the State. And most specifically because of this, the pain is so great, and the betrayal so piercing. You know this is not right, so before the State crumbles in your hands, for their sake, listen to the direction [of your heart], and do what is right. YOU KNOW WHAT IS RIGHT.

The Walls That Had the Last Word

Dear Soldier:
If only God would forgive you!!!

Gush Katif forever and ever

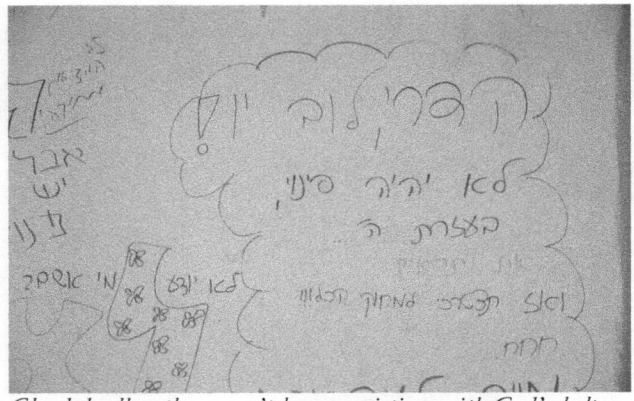

*Cloud dweller, there won't be any eviction, with God's help.
Then you will need to erase all [this]!!!
But there is eviction. Do you know who is guilty?*

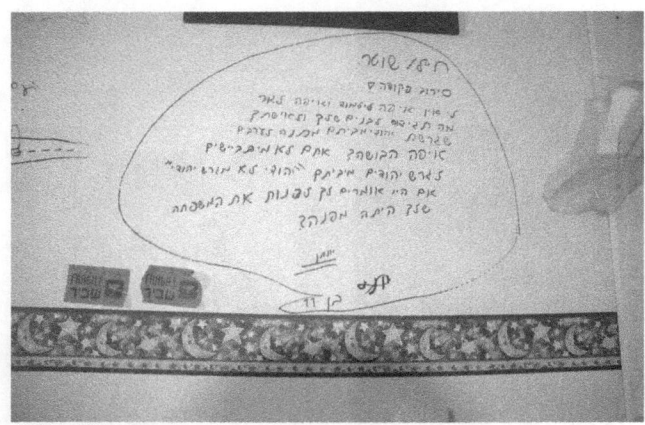

*Soldier/Police, refuse your orders!
I have nowhere to study, and nowhere to live. What will you tell your children, and your wife. That you expelled Jews from their house, [as] a present to the Arabs? Where is your shame [have you no shame]?
"A Jew doesn't expel another Jew."
If you were told to evict your family, would you do it?
Yonatan, aged 11*

The Walls That Had the Last Word

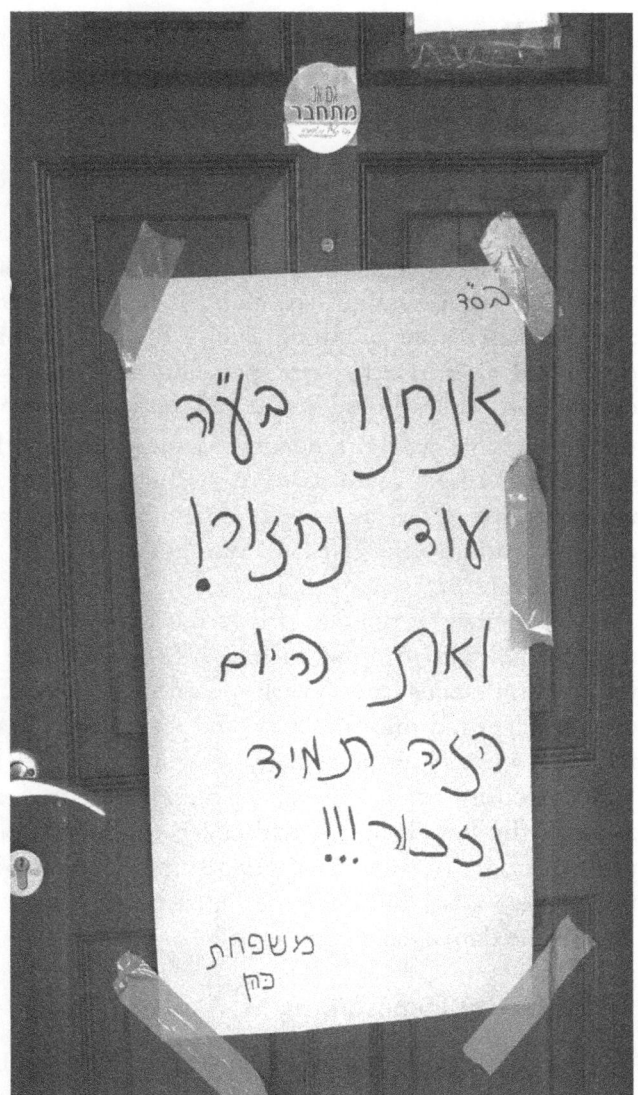

We, with the help of God, will yet return!
And this day we will always remember!!!
Cohen Family

A Personal Recollection of the Expulsion from Gush Katif

By Zimra Siegman-Schlessinger

October 15, 2005

It is now almost two months since the pogrom, although it has taken me until now to sit down and write about it. Actually, I haven't been able to sit down and read or write anything lately. I seem to have developed a short attention span and an inability to concentrate. I am afraid I will not remember everything – people have a tendency to forget things that are awful. What I seem to have disengaged from are my emotions. I feel as cool as a cucumber and suddenly I find myself bursting out into tears for no apparent reason.

Our personal tragedy is dwarfed by the national tragedy that will go down in Jewish history as one of the darkest stains the Jewish people have seen. A dictatorial prime minister managed, by undemocratic means, to make unprecedented cynical use of the Israeli security forces. Jewish soldiers aided the enemies of the Jewish nation and exiled the Jewish people from part of their Holy Land, thus encouraging further terrorism and endangering the entire state of Israel. The damage is yet to be told...

The Day of Deportation, My Personal Story

Neve Dekalim, Israel, August 17th, 2005 – The army announced that we would be permitted to attend *tefillot* [prayers] together at 11:00 a.m. and that they wouldn't start dragging people out until afterward. We hoped we could believe them and we went with the kids to the Yemenite Synagogue, where we once again poured out our tears and wrenching hearts to God, not knowing that His answer would eventually be "NO." We returned home at about 1:00 p.m. with our hearts in our mouths.

Shortly afterward, "Shiri," as she announced herself, came to the door. I looked through the peephole and saw the young brunette who had been sent to destroy our lives. I screamed at her and told her what I thought of her mission and that it was her obligation to refuse such orders and that she should leave, which she did, although she returned about an hour later. We told Menachem to tell her that his parents were not home (although we were right next to him) and that she should go away. She came back several more times in the following hours, and each time Menachem told her that we were not home.

We were exhausted. We hadn't slept the previous night, and we hadn't slept well for a long time. Every time we would doze off for a few seconds, a knock on the door would pull us back into the nightmare. Some man dressed in an orange vest marked "Rabbi" came a few times to try and convince Menachem to open the door. I don't think he actually was any sort of "Rabbi." He believed Menachem that we were not home, and I was appalled that he stooped so low as to try and convince a young child to do something against his parents' consent when he is home alone and frightened.

Somewhere between 5 and 6 p.m. "Shiri" returned with a great entourage. There were at least 40 soldiers with her. They all wore those pathetic blue vests and caps with Israeli flags – just so we could be sure we knew who sent them. They told Menachem they were going to break the door down even though his parents were not home. He informed them that his two-year-old little sister was standing near the door and that they could kill her by doing so, but this didn't seem to bother them, nor the "fact" (which in fact, was a lie) that his parents "were not home." Obviously, we held two-year-old Rachel away from the door, and as they started breaking in we moved to the kitchen and locked the door behind us. Within about 20 minutes, there was a repeat performance after a give-and-take between them and Menachem.

This time we moved into the girls' bedroom and locked the door. After about a half hour, they broke into that room too.

This is when our monologues began. Chananel and I poured our hearts (and words) out trying to make them see what a heinous crime they were partaking in, and they (as they were brainwashed to do) listened through us without saying a word. Shiri – the commanding deportation officer – asked us to board the bus, which was standing outside our house. We told her that we would not take any part in helping to commit this crime.

One by one, each of us and our five children were lifted by many soldiers and forced onto the bus, where there were more soldiers assigned to each passenger to make sure we wouldn't run off. It had just turned dark. According to Jewish law, it was already the following day, the 13th of Av. Only a week later would I realize that it was Simcha's birthday, which we would have spent together in our home as a festive event had we not been dragged off into the abyss.

The Bus Ride

The bus ride was a harrowing experience. Some of the men on the bus managed to kick out the windows and run. The soldiers ran after them, caught them, and brought them back to the bus. We were at complete standstills for hours at a time. The soldiers, who only moments earlier heartlessly dragged us out of our homes, suddenly became stewards and stewardesses – handing out mineral water and potato chips (and some sandwich that we wouldn't eat because the kashrut supervision was unclear). We would rather choke than take part in such a game. After we gave the children a drink we used the water to pour over the policemen who lined the streets on our way out. One of them got very angry and came up to the bus. Just then I realized – I had forgotten! Our "illegal" guests, whom we had hosted for the weeks preceding the expulsion, were hiding in our house! I quickly called them on their cell phones to make sure they weren't found. It made me feel good to know that they were still there. I hoped and prayed that this entire nightmare would be over and that we would be able to turn around soon and go back home. I said the travelers' prayer, and recited the words "and return us to our homes in peace," with lots of extra intent.

At around midnight we were dumped onto some street corner in Sderot. Did we find Yonatan Bassi [the head of the Disengagement administration] handing out refreshments? Of course not. There was bedlam – crying babies and children, dumbfounded adults, and no one knew who was to go where. Religious volunteers from Sderot organized a light dinner and some toys for the kids to play with until we would continue the next leg of our "journey." They helped us carry the children, who were half asleep, as well as the few belongings we managed to take with us. About an hour and a half later, we found ourselves on a bus going to a hotel in Natzeret Ilit. We arrived at about 5:00 a.m.

The Hotel

Did we find Yonatan Bassi at the hotel handing out refreshments? Of course not. There were a few good Jews who came out to help us with the kids and do whatever they could. But what on earth could they do?

Chananel and I were given a large room for all the kids and a room for us attached – with one mattress. This angered me so! It was already morning, neither of us had slept for one minute on the bus (Rachel had kicked and cried the entire way), and now, only one of us would be able to lie down. Someone brought us some shirts for the girls to sleep in – we had no pajamas – and we all "conked out" for a few hours.

When we got up, I took the kids to get some breakfast. The Arab who ran the dining hall said, "Breakfast is over." I disregarded him, went and took whatever I could find, and sat the kids on the floor in the hall and let them make a mess. Seeing all the Jews who were vacationing particularly troubled me. They were on their way to the swimming pool at the same time that the Jewish army was busy exiling the Jews from the holy land of Israel and from their homes.

The little ones kept running into the elevator. I was sure that there was no way I could continue like this. I realized that, geographically, I was so far away from where I needed to be. If we would receive permission to go back and pack up the house, how could we manage from so far away? How would we make such a long trip to the lawyer with the kids? We certainly couldn't leave them alone there, not even with a babysitter. They probably would think they would never see us again, in the same way that they were told that they would never go back home again!!

The Klavans

Yossi Klavan (formerly of Teaneck, NJ) was one of the first people I spoke with, not because I had the wherewithal to call anybody, but because he was persistent in calling me to find out what was going on. As soon as he knew where I was, he came to get us. He took a week off work to chauffeur us to anywhere we needed, and Leba, who had recently given birth, watched the kids and even took them to the pool a few times. We really didn't know where to start getting ourselves together. Yossi was very helpful. He suggested we shut the phone and electric line, which we hadn't thought of, and he started helping us work on getting permission to go into Gush Katif and pack up the house, which we had left untouched. All the while we continued to hope and pray that the nightmare would soon be over and that we would be able to go back home; but we started to understand that this would probably not be the case.

A few days later, Chananel was allowed to join a group that went into Gush Katif to pack. I was not allowed on the bus, as the strict orders prescribed that only one member per household could enter. After a long and dragged out journey, Chananel arrived in Neve Dekalim and was given 30 boxes. He was let off in the Neve Dekalim industrial zone with no car. He was informed that the truck was to arrive in about two hours. How can anyone pack an entire house in 30 boxes and in two hours?!?!?

Chananel walked home and cried. He called me on our phone (which hadn't been shut off). The whole house was standing and intact. The whole predicament was surreal. He was unable to pack. Yossi and I tried to find out how we could get some soldiers to go help. I spoke to MK Benny Elon and pleaded with him to find some way for the order to be given! There were tens of thousands of soldiers there! Why hadn't they been going from house to house to help pack?? Benny Elon explained that this was no mistake. He told me that they want to thoroughly break us. They want us to scramble around like the Jews in Europe who were told to "pack one bag quickly." Then they could have some reporters come and photograph a few soldiers "helping the settlers pack," as if this were the norm.

Brimo

Yossi spoke to the moving company. We asked them to postpone the move until the following day. He explained that we needed to bring in some people to pack. The mover told us we would have to get the OK from Brimo and accidentally gave us Brimo's number – something he apparently was not supposed to give out. We had no idea who Brimo was, but we later would find out that he was working for the Defense Ministry and in charge of allowing (or not allowing) certain moving companies to enter Gush Katif. We surmised that only those companies who gave him a nice "cut" were allowed in, which explained the outrageous price that was being asked for us to pay.

Yossi has a way with words — even with Brimo! I don't know how, but he managed to get Brimo to allow us to go into Gush Katif the following day to pack. We were instructed where to get the permission slip. It seemed too good to be true. Where was the catch? Brimo screamed at Yossi and made it amply clear that if he dared have any orange ribbons or stickers on his car or his body he would have him arrested as he had done to someone the previous day. He specified that he would not tolerate a sticker that said "Am Yisrael Chai!" As appalling as this all was, Yossi kept his cool and kept sweet-talking. Yossi arranged for us to go early the following morning, and Leba would baby-sit for my kids all day. Chananel decided to stay home in Neve Dekalim — this was illegal — until the next day when he would pack with us. Yossi's boys went all over to find as many boxes as they could. My parents did the same. Yossi arranged to go in two cars — his and Steve Leavitt's. We first had to go see Brimo...

We arrived at the "Brimo headquarters" a few minutes before 8 a.m., a few minutes before they had their act together, a few minutes before they closed the gate, a few minutes before they had the chance not to let us in. We had tons of divine assistance all along the way. They had no intention to give us permission to enter after all. We were yelled at by everyone who saw us, including Brimo himself: "WHO LET YOU IN HERE?!?!?" Since we were there already, and since no buses were being allowed into Gush Katif that day, Brimo did an "act of kindness" so he could feel good about himself for the next year and he kept his word and allowed us in. He gave us a slip of paper and entered us into the computer that showed we had permission to go in.

We were told to stay in a Defense Ministry convoy that was going into Gush Katif, which we did, even though they were driving so slowly that we could have probably walked faster. Just as we arrived at the Kissufim checkpoint, a particularly hotheaded (and bloodthirsty) police officer violently stopped us and forced us to leave the convoy. He would not listen to what we had to say, and refused to look at our permission slip. He also refused to ask the army officer in the car ahead of us, as I pleaded, about our being part of the convoy. He was going to have some FUN!!! Just as he was about to beat the living daylights out of Yossi, the army officer from the car ahead of us miraculously came to our rescue and said we were with them, leaving the poor policeman to wait for some other unfortunate person with whom to have his fun.

Packing

When we arrived at the gate of Neve Dekalim, we had to wait almost a half hour until we were allowed in. Shortly afterwards, I was back home. I went into the boys' room and burst into tears. Everyone started working immediately. I bothered them and was of no help whatsoever. Yossi, who had never done anything like this in his life, took apart all my closets with Steve and his friend (I forget his name). Shabie from Ginot Shomron worked like a stick of energy almost non-stop. They packed everything in about 11 hours. And I really mean everything – even the windows, doors, and light bulbs! I was soon to find out that I would be ripped off by the moving company big-time – about NIS 23,000 worth of rip-off. I would also learn later that others who used this company had found their belongings ruined, stolen, or vandalized. I still have no idea what condition my things are in, wherever they may be.

Back to Yossi's House

Yossi and Leba continued to take us wherever we needed to go – to the lawyer in Tel Aviv, to buy sandals for the boys and shirts for Chananel, to develop our photographs of what we managed to take during the eviction. Yossi even took us to visit Chananel's great-aunt in Ramat Hasharon. We really had no idea where we were headed, though.

I got in touch with Rabbi Yom Tov Zilberman who runs the main branch of the schools that the boys were attending (which we had been so pleased with), and asked him where would be appropriate for the boys to continue. He asked me which area we were interested in. I knew that at this time I could only see myself continuing the battle over the land of Israel. We are the antithesis of this government, who will do anything for a buck. They will sell their souls and everything that is holy for money. We, on the other hand, are willing to lose everything for what we believe in. After we spoke with Rabbi Zilberman, I began arranging visits to our new prospective homes – Hebron, Beit El, and Gush Dolev-Talmonim. Yossi was very helpful with this too, as he has contacts everywhere, and was very instrumental in getting me in touch with the right people.

The Schlep

We began schlepping the kids on a long journey and we didn't know when it would end. We used my parents' house in Beit Shemesh as our base and went from there to Hebron, Jerusalem, Beit El, and Gush Talmonim. We slept in many different places and wasted a ton of money on transportation. At one point, my cousin Atara from Beit Shemesh came and insisted we borrow her car. I was very uneasy about it, but she was persistent. Without this great help I can't imagine how we ever would have been able to get ourselves together so quickly.

Haresha

After seeing different schools (the kids participated in classes in Hebron and Beit El), we decided that the school in Neriya would be most appropriate for the boys. We also found a good school for Simcha in Dolev. (These places are in Gush Dolev-Talmonim.) We had made up our minds about the general area we wanted to be in based on the children's education, but we still had no home and no job.

After seeing the area, our hearts pulled us in the direction of Haresha, a small community of 30 families on a hilltop near the boys' school (five minutes away). Unfortunately, the Israeli government does not recognize the existence of this place, although the army does. It is the most vital strategic asset the army has in the area, as it is 900 meters high and overlooks the entire area, including Ramallah. I wouldn't want to know what catastrophe could happen, God forbid, if Haresha got into the wrong hands.

Most of the homes in Haresha are trailers. They range from 45 to 90 sq. meters. It is not very easy to live in such conditions, but the people in Haresha are worth sacrificing some earthly comforts for. We decided that we would like to live in Haresha and we requested a caravan. We had no time for bureaucracy. I explained to the absorption committee that I wanted my kids in school on time the next day like every other normal kid in the country. I also explained that if they could not yet arrange a caravan, I had been planning on sleeping on the grass. After this meeting, I took the kids to the neighboring town (Kiryat Sefer, about 20 minutes away) to get dinner. There, we received a call from the absorption committee of Haresha announcing that they had a meeting and we were accepted to their community. They also said that there was an empty 60-meter caravan available for us. We were happy. I asked if they could arrange to have some mattresses in it for us and they said they would. When we arrived, we found that they had not only cleaned the place from top to bottom, but they had set up beds for all of us with sheets, pillows, towels, and blankets, as well as a table and chairs, shelves, a stovetop, a microwave, a toaster oven, some food, and even a refrigerator (borrowed from the kindergarten, the rest from our neighboring families). They got us a new set of dishes and ritually immersed them! They set up books and toys for the kids and a tape recorder with some tapes. They even put toothpaste, soap, and shampoo in the bathroom!

For two days, meals were prepared by our neighbors and sent to us. Our neighbors continue to take care of our laundry until now. Haresha has a very nice kindergarten and beautifully run day-care facility for the little ones, and there is a very nice *kollel* for Chananel at the foot of the mountain (less than a five-minute drive).

We don't yet have anywhere to bring our belongings (if they still exist), but we are still working on it. We might be able to rent another caravan for our things. In the meantime, we are being charged NIS 2,000 a month for what they call storage.

I haven't found a job yet, but I am hopeful about next year. Schools don't leave themselves "high and dry" for an English teacher waiting to be evicted from her home.

I am trying to collect unemployment, although the bureaucracy is endless, and I recently found out that the amount of money paid is barely enough to starve on. Chananel also cannot find a job before next September, which puts us in a very difficult situation. We have no source of income, and therefore we have not paid the kids' tuition, nor our rent, utilities, or anything else. We have not seen one dime from the government, even though we have filled out all the forms they asked us to via a lawyer. If the government had spent a fraction of the money they spent lying and claiming we were all compensated on actually compensating us, we would all be millionaires.

"A Barbaric Act" – The Destruction of the Synagogues in Gush Katif

By Ali Waked on behalf of Ynetnews.com

September 12, 2005

Foreign Minister Silvan Shalom slammed the burning of Gaza synagogues, characterizing it as "a barbaric act by people who have no respect for holy places.

"This statement by Abu Mazen, as if the buildings lost their sanctity, is misplaced. The Palestinians did not invest any effort in preserving the synagogues and have thus failed their first mission," he said. "We've seen acts by terror groups manifested through severe vandalism.

"The responsibility is placed on the Palestinians. Abu Mazen must remember the eyes of the entire world are turned to the Strip today and the anarchy threatens him and his people more than it threatens us."

"The burning of synagogues in the Gaza Strip is a demonstration of Palestinian barbarity, with the Palestinian Authority, as usual, showing a complete inability to respond," Knesset Member Shaul Yahalom (National Religious Party) said.

"This is the ultimate proof of the terrible future we can expect from the terrorists of Gaza," he said.

Meanwhile, Knesset Defense and Foreign Affairs Committee Chairman Yuval Steinitz said the burning of synagogues in Gaza proves "we have no genuine, responsible partner for peace on the other side, but at most, a partner for excuses.

"Israel must initiate a diplomatic, public relations offensive that would expose the Palestinian government's true face to the world."

Synagogues Set on Fire

Early Monday, a Palestinian mob raided the evacuated Gaza settlements and proceeded to sow destruction and vandalize them. Four synagogues – in Morag, Netzanim, Neve Dekalim, and Kfar Darom – were torched.

Around 2:30 a.m., a Palestinian mob from Khan Yunis raided the settlement of Morag and set the community's synagogue on fire. The masses were holding PLO and Hamas flags, and they fired shots in the air and fireworks in celebration.

"This is only the first step of the liberation. Tomorrow we'll liberate all of Palestine," the Palestinians yelled. Meanwhile, youngsters looted whatever they could find, including tables, chairs, and other furniture.

Palestinian police officers were stunned in the face of the mob and were unable to contain it. Palestinian officers complained that the force deployed at the community was too small, about 300 troops, and could not handle the rioters.

Later, the masses reached Netzarim as well, where they shattered the deserted synagogue's windows and attempted to set it on fire. Palestinian police forces at the scene attempted to stop the vandals, but to no avail. Palestinians made their way to the synagogue's rooftop, held up flags, and yelled out, "We don't want anything to remain that will remind us of the occupation."

In Kfar Darom, a mob also set the synagogue on fire.

In Neve Dekalim, a synagogue that served as a yeshiva was also set on fire. The large building was slightly damaged by the thick smoke that rose above the area.

"The Israelis destroy our homes and our mosques. Now is our turn to destroy theirs," said one of the rioters, Ahmed.

PA to Raze Synagogues

Early Monday, PA Chairman Mahmoud Abbas issued a statement saying synagogues in evacuated settlements will be destroyed by the Palestinian Authority.

"The Israelis left behind empty structures that served as synagogues in the past," the statement read. "But they removed all religious artifacts from there and therefore they are no longer holy places." Earlier, PA officials blasted Israel's decision to leave the Gaza Strip synagogues intact, and said the move placed the Palestinians in a "no win" situation.

The Story of Roz and Paul Schneid, Part Two – Homeless and Wandering
By Naomi Ragen

This article originally appeared in Moment Magazine.

Paul and Roz, who are leading members of their community, stayed with their neighbors until soldiers – members of the air force in which Paul's son serves as a senior officer – came knocking on their door. They had asked for containers and received them. (By the way, these containers are costing the settlers $2,000 each, and they will be charged an additional $1,500 for moving costs. All the compensation owed to them will also be taxed! And they are not getting much.) The night before, in order to spare the young soldiers as much pain as possible, they did the packing themselves. When the soldiers knocked on the door of their home, they said, "I'm so sorry. I know how hard this must be for you." A group of officers came to call on the family because of Paul's son. They embraced, and then they left the house together for the last time.

Silently, they marched with their neighbors to the synagogue, the same synagogue whose Rabbi was brutally murdered by Palestinian terrorists two years ago. This is no bedroom community. This is not a neighborhood, as most of us understand it. This is an extended family whose members have sat shiva in each other's homes and banded together to help when thousands of rockets fell in their backyards and on their roofs. They have been in a furnace of terror together and have emerged welded into one cohesive unit: Sephardim and Ashkenazim, teachers and farmers, businessmen and grocery store owners. They love each other. And they love the soldiers.

At the synagogue, the soldiers and settlers suddenly put their arms around each other's shoulders and sang songs of the land of Israel, each quietly wiping away tears. This went on for two hours. Paul was asked to speak. He tried so hard to be upbeat and hopeful. He spoke of their history together, how they had come from all different backgrounds, how they were a microcosm of Israel. He looked at the soldiers and told them they were one. "When we slip our hands together and hold each other, we can't fight. We can only build." They could destroy the buildings and take away the land. But the spirit within the community, the oneness, the eagerness to continue building the land was unquenched within them. The community asked only one thing: not to be separated, not to be sent to different apartments in different cities, to be left together as a unit.

They had been saying this from the beginning to everyone who would listen. And as any psychologist would tell you, they needed each other to get through this.

They were loaded peacefully onto buses. It was then that the nightmare began for the wonderful people of Netzer Chazani. No stops were made for bathrooms. They were on the bus for six hours. At their request, they went first to the Kotel.

Yeshivat Hakotel gave them a place to sleep. The next morning, according to the "plans" of the Disengagement Administration (SELA), the community was sent up to Chispin in the Golan Heights, a five-hour drive away. They were originally told they could stay there until September 1st. But on Saturday night, after all they'd been through, they were told by the hotel administration that they needed to get out of their rooms to make way for other guests on Sunday morning! They were offered dilapidated dorm rooms, without air conditioning, instead. Fearing for the health of their children, they refused. Overwrought, tempers flared and the entire community decided to march back to their homes in Netzer Chazani. That's where they are now, on the road, feeling exhausted, angry, and heartbroken.

Paul and Roz aren't with them. Paul needed to have chemotherapy today. But when he got to the hospital, he was told that he needed to pick up his vital drugs from the pharmacy. When he got to the pharmacy, he was told that he needed a letter from his local clinic. He patiently explained that he no longer had a local clinic (just as he explained to the supermarket cashier that he had no telephone number to put on his credit card receipt...). It took him three hours to straighten it out. Sick, tired, jobless, and homeless, he and his wife are waiting to see what will happen next, and where they will sleep tonight.

I have heard some people say: "Well, what do people expect when they didn't make any plans? When they refused to cooperate?"

I know it's hard for most people to understand, but they weren't worried about themselves. They were concerned about the state of mind of the community if they went off and fended for themselves, concerned about setting an example that would encourage everyone to go their own way, helping to destroy the only thing left: the community and its spirit.

They are a rare, endangered species: idealists. Like beautiful old houses and rare animals, the special community of Netzer Chazani must be preserved. That's all its people want. Not luxury hotels. Not huge houses with swimming pools. They want to be together in a place that will afford them their basic necessities. SELA, whose incompetence is a national disgrace, suggested sending them to Eilat (six hours away, in hotels that are empty for a reason: 45 degree summer heat). They also offered to send them to the Dead Sea (ditto). And then they sent them to the Golan, without bothering to check how long the hotel could host them.

There is so much empty land all over the Galilee. Why couldn't they have simply put a caravan park there? "We couldn't force people, decide for them where to go. And they weren't talking to us," SELA has been whining. They remind me of the rapist who tells the victim, "If you only wouldn't have struggled so much, you would have made it so much easier for yourself."

For shame. For shame. For shame. For shame. For shame.

A Synagogue or a Bathroom?
By Paula R. Stern

www.paulasays.com

September, 2005

It's hard to believe that only a few weeks ago, I had an idea to try to save a synagogue in Gush Katif and bring it to Maaleh Adumim. So much has happened since then, so much destroyed, so much lost, and so many lives changed. The physical communities of Gush Katif have been erased, the synagogues destroyed by Palestinian mobs; and worst of all are the continued efforts to break the spirit of the people who were expelled from Gush Katif and northern Samaria.

The people, the extraordinary and precious people, continue to receive horrendous treatment while the nation is given lies by the Sharon government and his Bassi puppet. Barely any of the refugees have received compensation payments; most are denied access to their possessions unless they agree to pay thousands of shekels to the shipping company that the government hired to move their equipment. Most have been moved several times in an ongoing attempt to break up the unity of the communities. The greenhouses that might have been used to better the lives of Palestinians lie in ruins, looted and destroyed by the same Palestinian mobs who felt no shame in torching our holy places.

Only a month ago, I asked a simple question: if you could save one building in your community, which would it be? And then I explained that, for the community of Nachalat Yehuda in Maaleh Adumim, that one building was a small study hall and synagogue that belonged to a yeshiva in Moshav Katif.

On September 8th, as I was returning from a meeting in Tel Aviv, I drove on the main highway, knowing time was running out. In the evening, Gush Katif would be sealed off; within days it would be abandoned. Most of it had already been destroyed. We'd received assurances and promises for days that the little synagogue was safe and would be moved. It would be ours to honor, to use, to hold until Moshav Katif wanted it back.

Yet the hour was late and we still did not have any concrete idea as to when the building would be removed. We started receiving conflicting information and we were worried that in all the confusion, the army would leave the building behind to share the same fate as the larger synagogues that could not be removed easily. These were the ones that the Sharon government was willing to see burned and desecrated, rather than delay the mad capitulation a little longer in order to remove them properly or gain international guarantees of safety to protect the sanctity of these structures.

In several phone calls, the Religious Affairs Department of the Prime Minister's office was promising us that the synagogue was fine and would be moved within hours. But a moving company that had been in and out of Gush Katif for days was telling us that the building was gone, probably moved already and likely lost among hundreds of others.

My mind filled with possibilities as I drove on the main Jerusalem-Tel Aviv highway until I got to the Latrun junction, halfway home. But, instead of continuing straight on towards Jerusalem, I exited to the right – south to Gaza … for the last time. I would try to enter Gush Katif, I decided. The mystery of the synagogue's status would end now. Either it had been moved or it was there waiting. Time had run out.

It seemed ridiculous that no one knew, and yet at the same time, with Sharon's frantic dash for the border, it seemed entirely logical that amid the chaos, we might lose the synagogue. I contacted the Religious Affairs Department again as I drove south.

"It's there," he told me yet again.

"We want to move it," I told him.

"We're doing the best we can," he told me.

"Give me permission to move it," I responded. "Let me tell the moving company to pick it up and take it now. We'll pay." Anything. Please, let us just save this one synagogue. Don't let bureaucracy destroy our one chance to save a synagogue. He debated for a moment and then agreed. "Take it."

"Can you get me permission to enter Gaza?" I asked. But this was too much for him. "I can't even go in anymore," he answered. Less than 30 minutes away and still with no clear plan, I called a friend who had secured passes into Gaza in the past. "Get me in there," I pleaded with him.

While my friend worked on the pass, I continued to drive south, passing Sderot, knowing that soon more rockets would fall. Tomorrow would be for worries about Sderot; today was for a small synagogue crying out to me. I called the moving company. "It isn't there," he told me yet again.

"I'm going in if I can get a pass. I have permission for you to move it."

"It isn't there."

Synagogue or a Bathroom?

Perhaps it was the tears he could hear in my voice, perhaps it was the fear that time was running out. Whatever he heard in my voice, he relented. "Go in," he told me. "Call me when you get there. I'll come and get it out if it is there."

The rest of the trip, short though it was, was done in silence. I didn't let my mind think too far ahead. There were very few people left in Gaza; most of the communities had already been destroyed. I already knew what the rubble and desolation looked like. I thought I was as prepared as I could be.

When I arrived at the Kissufim Crossing, the last checkpoint, the soldiers told me I didn't have permission to enter. A series of calls back and forth produced nothing. I waited; my friend tried all channels. While he was calling, a soldier walked over and gave me a pass. "I'm in," I told my friend. "I'm in."

I drove straight to Moshav Katif. The last time I'd been here, only a week before, the houses still stood, activity was everywhere. The main synagogue had been emptied and the small synagogue we'd found still had benches, a kitchen, the Holy Ark, and books inside.

Now, the houses were gone, years and years of building reduced to rubble. It was hard to find the right location, but in the end I found the row of buildings. The first had been the dining room; it lay in ruins. The third building had contained bathrooms and offices; it had been removed to a safe location, leaving only flattened earth behind. Amidst the remnants of people's homes, I mourned neither of these buildings.

But sadly, the second building, the only synagogue that we might have been able to save, had been destroyed as well. It is entirely likely that the bulldozer driver never realized that it was a synagogue he was destroying – another victim of Sharon's cowardly exit from Gaza.

I was alone in Katif. Only the soldiers stood guard at the gate, but they too would soon be evacuated. I stood looking at the ruins of the small synagogue. It's impossible to describe the anguish I felt, the feeling that we had failed it. I had imagined it so many times resting on the hills of Maaleh Adumim, facing Jerusalem and filled with the voices of our congregation. We would have covered it in Jerusalem stone, but we would still have known where it had come from. I had never imagined it lying at my feet in ruins, the walls smashed, the roof mangled and collapsed.

Behind me, there was the large synagogue that had been the gathering place of the entire community. But this small building had only been used by a high school. It had been overlooked completely when the issue of the synagogues' future was raised with the Israeli courts and so it was initially left behind.

Compared to the destruction awaiting the magnificent and majestic synagogues, this one would be insignificant. All of Israel would cry for what was to be done. Throughout the world, supporters of Israel and those who believe in respecting the religion and holy sites of others would mourn the barbaric torching and destruction of the large synagogues of Gush Katif.

But there was no one left to mourn for this building, and so I mourned for its loss standing there alone in Katif. It was nothing compared to the larger, permanent structures that would soon be desecrated by the Palestinians, I told myself. It was nothing compared to the homes of 9000 people, miniscule in the scale of destruction; and yet I mourned for it as a symbol of something so much larger.

The people of Gush Katif, like the small synagogue, are too often thought of as insignificant in the larger picture of Israel's future. But what was done to them cannot be forgotten. We cannot forget or forgive the Sharon government's robbing people of their communities and livelihoods in exchange for more rocket attacks, more infiltrations, and continued threats and incitement

Take off your orange ribbons, I am told almost daily. No, I reply, not until the last Gush Katif refugee is settled in his home; not until I understand why our government surrendered to terrorism and allowed Jewish synagogues to be desecrated.

And deep inside myself, I will always remember that a small synagogue was destroyed while the bathroom next to it was saved. If you could save one building in your community, which would it be? The Sharon government answered: a bathroom.

And Even the Dead – To Unbury a Son
By Rachel Saperstein

March 7, 2005

There are 46 graves in the cemetery in Gush Katif. They are the graves of loved ones – parents, spouses, and children. Each grave tells a story of bravery under fire, an accident, or a severe illness.

During my years in Neve Dekalim, I began to know the people buried in the sandy earth of Gush Katif. I began to know the families and the stories of their loved ones.

Three sons lie under the earth of Gush Katif:

A Naval Hero

The late Yochanan Hilberg was buried in the Katif cemetery by his parents, Sammy and Bryna. Yochanan, an outstanding naval commando, was killed in Lebanon on a secret mission. A film, "You Can't Cry Underwater," was produced by the Ulpana Neve Dekalim Communications Department. It tells the poignant story of how Sammy and Bryna coped with their son's death. The family raised money to build the Yochanan Youth Club in Moshav Netzer Hazani, his home. A "Run for Yochanan" takes place each Chanukah, when his IDF friends, family, and community youth join together to remember Yochanan.

Yochanan Hilberg is buried in the Gush Katif cemetery. With the threat of expulsion, his bones, his gravestone, all traces of this hero are to be unburied.

Says Bryna, "My son was killed for his country and now the country wants to kill him again."

Itai's Legacy

Udi and Shlomo Yulis have a son in the Gush Katif cemetery. Itai was 14 and a half years old when he died after a three-year battle with leukemia. Itai had been active in the Bnei Akiva youth movement. His family donated a Sefer Torah and a religious library to the Bnei Akiva Center in Neve Dekalim. Each year, a basketball tournament is held in Itai's memory.

A large picture of a smiling Itai greets you when you enter the Yulis home.

"He fought his illness with courage and belief in G-d. He bestowed this courage and this trust in the Almighty as his legacy to us," said Shlomo.

"We were told – indirectly, as the government has not approached us – that we have two choices: to carry his remains to a home we know not where, or leave it here in Gush Katif in the 'care' of the Arabs.

"I was always a member of the Likud," says Shlomo. "The Likud believed in the sanctity of the Land of Israel. Now, we are to be expelled with my son's bones. What Zionist education do we give to our children?" he whispers, close to tears. "We look to the legacy of Itai and his strong acceptance of G-d's decrees. This gives us the courage to continue and hold on."

Killed by Our Own

Elkana Goobi was 21 the night he drove his older brother Boaz to his army base. His younger brother sat in the rear. The boys were still in their

Shabbat clothes – white shirt, black pants, white kippah.

They heard gunfire on the road. Arabs were shooting at the passing vehicles. Elkana, a sharpshooter in an elite army unit, stopped their car. Pulling out their rifles, the brothers opened fire on the Arabs, forcing them to flee, leaving behind a trail of grenades. An army jeep mistook the brothers for the terrorists and ran Elkana down, killing him. Boaz raised his arms, screaming, "We're Jews!"

Elkana, a natural leader, a boy of strong personal character, died for *Kiddush Hashem*, the sanctity of the Lord, says his brother.

Miri and Moshe Goobi have lived in Neve Dekalim for 25 years. The family donated a Torah scroll and a magnificent lighting fixture for their synagogue in Elkana's name. A Passover *haggada* was published with added pictures, letters, and anecdotes from Elkana's friends.

"We never knew the extent of his friendships or his *chessed*, kindness to others. He lived a full life in his short years," says Miri, trying to smile. "I go to his grave. I care for the flowers around it.

"No one, but no one, will take his grave away from here. I will protect it with my life!"

"The army killed him once and the government wants to unbury him. How many times can a family sit *shiva* [the traditional Jewish seven-day mourning period] for a son?" cries Elkana's father.

To Unbury a Son

Photo provided by Paula R. Stern
The cemetery in Gush Katif

Photo provided by Pinchas Orbach
The coffins taken to Jerusalem before reaching their final destination

Photo provided by Pinchas Orbach
A coffin on its journey from Jerusalem to re-burial

The Day of the Expulsion
Photos Provided by Debbie Rosen

Soldiers moving in

Soldiers waiting to evacuate a home

The Expulsion from Gush Katif

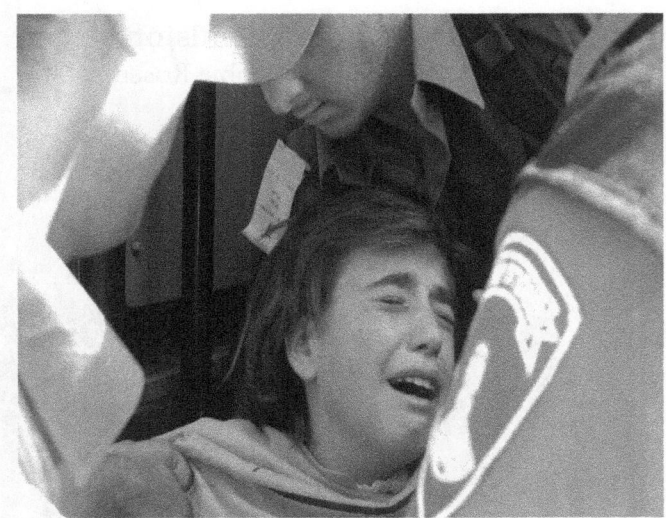

Soldiers carrying out a boy from his home

The Day of the Expulsion

THE EXPULSION FROM GUSH KATIF

A soldier and settler embrace

Soldiers escort people out

THE DAY OF THE EXPULSION

Soldiers gather, ready to evacuate

The sign on the car reads "Expelled Jew"

Stickers protesting the Disengagement

The sound of the blood of our brothers cries to us from the land. (See: Genesis 4:10)

THE EXPULSION FROM GUSH KATIF

Those being evicted pray

The Torah Scrolls are carried out for the final time

Photo provided by Paula R. Stern
A shul before the expulsion

Photo provided by Paula R. Stern
The same shul after it has been dismantled

Section Three:

The Aftermath

The Aftermath
Photos provided by Debbie Rosen

A bulldozer reduces a house to rubble

A bulldozer tears through the rubble

A home after it has been destroyed

After the bulldozers have destroyed the homes

The Aftermath

A tree left standing in the rubble

THE EXPULSION FROM GUSH KATIF

A family house sign is all that remains

After the Expulsion
By Rabbi Yosef Elnekaveh

We arrived at the hotel in Jerusalem at night, feeling extremely drained and exhausted. The families had been arriving gradually at the hotels, from Tuesday night until Friday afternoon. When we got there, the residents of Allon Shvut, French Hill, and other communities warmly greeted us with fruit and cold drinks. They had clearly put themselves out to look after us. There was a feeling that the heroes of Gush Katif had arrived and that we should receive warm, heartfelt hospitality. To me, our fellow Jews seemed rather like the Jerusalemites of ancient times who would go out with their baskets of the first fruits, trumpets, and *shofars*.

Many people were deeply moved and they came up to the hall to pray along with us. On Friday night, a hotel guest from France sat next to me, and when we started to sing the prayers to a Carlebach tune, he could not find his place because he was familiar with only the Sephardic liturgy.

I told him that there was another service outside that he would find much easier to follow. He thought for a moment and then answered in heavily accented Hebrew, "*Non, non*, no, I understand, er…not really, but it doesn't matter because I am honored to pray with you, the residents of Gush Katif!"

During the Shabbat meal, when we felt as if the usual melodies were sticking in our throats, Esther Bazak stood up and told us that her husband died on a Friday. Later on, when the family got up from the *shiva* for Shabbat, she told her children to remember that in spite of their feelings, that day was still Shabbat.

"Right now we may be in mourning, but we still all need to sing," she said. And in response, all of us – especially the teenagers, who had such an amazing spirit – started to sing. From then on, the melodies flowed.

At dawn the following morning, we were concerned that no one would be awake in time to join us for the early minyan that we had been running for years. However, we were very fortunate, and the early service took place as usual.

We were joined by a young man who had immigrated to Israel only recently from the United States. I asked him if he wanted to say a few words, and he began to speak in English. Visibly moved, he burst into tears and said, "I came here to see you heroes. I knew and saw what they did to you, and I was sure that you would be broken by it. But here you are, singing and still believing." Suddenly, he cried out, "Master of the Universe! Look at your children, rejoicing on Shabbat. But you are homeless!!!"

And we, the residents of Gush Katif, were not even thinking at that point about the fact that we were indeed homeless. When the first family arrived at its temporary caravan accommodation, the mother told us that until that day they had felt very much like exiles.

"But now we have a table, and there is home-cooked food. When I saw my husband sitting on his chair at the head of the table on Shabbat, I finally understood that once again he is the master of a house," she said.

My Neighbor from Bombay
By Shifra Shomron

This article appeared in www.english.katif.net

September 28, 2005 (24 Elul, 5765)

Nitzan Caravilla Site

Several days ago, in her 60-square meter caravilla, Simcha Shimshon passed away. Simcha used to be my neighbor. Back in beautiful Neve Dekalim, she lived only three houses away.

I never knew much about her life story. She was from Bombay, India, and she had only one child – a grown son who lived with his family in the adjoining agricultural community of Gadid. Simcha loved her only son, daughter-in-law, and grandchildren. She constantly kept pictures of them with her.

I had often seen her slowly shuffle to a neighbor's house in order to sit in a comfortable living room or lively kitchen, and watch the children play and tease each other or listen to the grownups' conversation. In her own house, Simcha always kept the television or radio on, but I am sure that the elderly lady from Bombay found it much more interesting and enjoyable to sit in her Yemenite neighbor's house and follow the family dynamics.

You see, Simcha loved life and, in her limited way, tried to be a part of ours and our neighbors' lives.

There were times I would walk over (reluctantly, I shamefully admit) and help her around her house; I would sweep her floor, adjust the living room blinds, change the bedding, and dump the garbage. She always greeted me with a smile, shuffled around, and followed my actions. When I finished she would present me with a toffee candy or two.

My mother would encourage all of us children to spend time with our elderly neighbor but, aside from my three youngest siblings, none of us really did so. Simcha's attempts to sit in *our* living room didn't work out, despite my mother's willingness, since the rest of us were not comfortable with this breach of our privacy.

Yet Simcha was happy – and busy. During the week she would sit in her Yemenite neighbor's house, watch the children merrily playing in the playground right across the street, do arts and crafts at the Golden Age Center in Neve Dekalim, attend Hebrew ulpan classes at the bomb shelter next door to her house, watch television, and for Shabbatot and holidays she always went to her son's house and visited her grandchildren. She had her own house on a quarter of a *dunam*. She was independent, active, and alert.

But Prime Minister Sharon's "Disengagement Plan" changed things.

Like all other Gush Katif residents, Simcha was banished from her house. Her devoted son managed to procure a caravilla for her in the Nitzan caravilla site. Since she was from Neve Dekalim, she was placed in the Neve Dekalim section.

Simcha was very sad. She didn't like her new situation. She didn't know where her old neighbors were (most of them being scattered in hotels) and she didn't have with what to occupy herself. The bus driver she knew and liked, who used to drive her to the Golden Age Center back in Neve Dekalim, was now unemployed like most former Gush Katif residents, and ... she *yearned* to return to her house in the Gush.

Seeking to improve his mother's situation, her son arranged for her to move to a caravilla in the Gadid section – in fact, to live right next door to him. So, yet again, Simcha's belongings were packed up and moved. It must have been very stressful for her.

Monday, 22nd Elul (September 26, 2005), Simcha either fell and hit her head or suffered from a stroke. Death was practically instantaneous.

Such was Simcha's demise. The last thing she had been doing before her death was sitting on her couch and flipping through a picture album of her grandchildren. Former Gush Katif residents came to Nitzan from the various hotels in order to escort Simcha to her final resting place and comfort the grieving family.

I'm sorry that I never knew more about Simcha. Not even her exact age is known (she was in her mid-80s); they didn't have such documents in Bombay. She was clearly a well-educated woman, fluent in both her Indian dialect and the English language. Looking at her fine facial features and at how she carried herself, my mother would say that she must have been very beautiful when she was younger.

Oh, Simcha! Happiness seems to have forsaken us for a time – but for a time only. Joy *shall* be ours once again!

And may your memory be blessed.

Gush Katif Revisited
By Esther Marcus

"When we first arrived here, the Arabs told us we were crazy," recalls Rivka Goldmintz, a former resident of Gush Katif. "'Nothing will grow on this soil,' they said, and they assured us that we would go back to our cities in a year or two."

But Rivka and many others stayed for a very long time, as long as they possibly could. They built beautiful homes and vibrant, healthy communities, as well as schools and playgrounds for their children. In the process, they transformed a "yellow desert" into a flowering and fertile land.

It's hard not to cry, and we all know why – images of dream homes in flames; fathers, mothers, teenagers, and grandparents carried off their land by Jewish soldiers; beloved family members unburied to be reburied elsewhere; and families sitting *shiva* again. And, of course, this was only the beginning of the pain and loss. Nine months later, these very accomplished, independent, strong, and ideological people are depressed and mourning. While tremendous preparation and attention was given to their forced removal from the land, very little thought was devoted to what they would need after this major upheaval in their lives.

Indeed, Rabbi Yosef Tzvi Rimon recalls that when he was asked by some of the rabbis from Gush Katif, two days before the actual evacuation, to go to the Jerusalem hotels intended to receive the evacuees, he found that nothing had been prepared for them.

"These are families with seven or eight children, and there was no place for them to do their laundry,"

Rabbi Rimon explains. "There was nothing for their children to do in these hotels – no games, no activities, no room for them to play. And the *kashrus* in many of the hotels was not up to the standards of the incoming families. Other than dropping them off at the hotel, there was no real plan for their future."

Effects of Expulsion

Rabbi Rimon, the Chief Rabbi of Allon Shvut and an educator in Har Tzion (the yeshiva of Gush Etzion), took it upon himself to start organizing. He mobilized his own community. The night that the evacuees were to arrive at the hotel, Rabbi Rimon and his community of doctors, lawyers, accountants, and teachers were waiting with open arms.

"We stayed with them all night," Rabbi Rimon recalls. And the community support has continued. For a while the focus was on clothes and food. But as time went on, Rabbi Rimon recognized that the most critical issue was unemployment.

"People who walked into hotels with strength and confidence were becoming very depressed," Rabbi Rimon recalls. Many of the Gush Katif residents, he explains, were self-employed. A significant number were farmers, others were storekeepers or proprietors of other small businesses. Uprooted from their land and livelihoods, living in close quarters with spouses and no job to go to, the stress level was, and for many continues to be, very high.

Unsurprisingly, the impact on domestic life has been extremely trying. Marriages are strained; since the expulsion, ten divorce proceedings have been initiated. Children are also suffering; sleeplessness, bedwetting, difficult adjustments in new schools, inability to concentrate, and other post-traumatic behavior have been commonly diagnosed among children and teenagers.

Looking for Jobs

The lack of employment and income is probably the most devastating consequence for these formerly self-sufficient adults, states Rabbi Rimon.

Once again undeterred by the impossibility of the task, Rabbi Rimon started looking for jobs. He mobilized volunteers from his own community – 250 professionals – who were ready to help. They took it upon themselves to help write resumes and to mentor, setting aside time to call two to three people every day to encourage and motivate them to find work.

By the end of Elul, one and a half months after the evacuations, Rabbi Rimon found jobs for dozens of people. Some of these jobs were temporary, but today, he says, many of these same people have permanent work. On the eve of Rosh Hashanah, Rabbi Rimon recognized another opportunity in the timing of events. He began making connections between Gush Katif evacuees and businesses selling *sukkot* and the Four Species. The idea was very successful. It gave people with nothing to do a chance to earn money and a focus on something purposeful in their otherwise distressing situation.

His success, combined with the tremendous need, has led Rabbi Rimon to found JobKatif. Today, this group, a genuine grassroots organization, has succeeded in finding 120 people jobs. This translates into income for over 600 people. Over the last few months, JobKatif has evolved into a multifaceted organization. There is now a website, www.jobkatif.org.il, which continually updates job listings. In addition, Rabbi Rimon succeeded in pushing though legislation in the Knesset that offers companies government-sponsored financial incentives to hire evacuees from Gush Katif.

JobKatif has also raised money to finance professional retraining courses. Many former Gush Katif residents worked in agriculture, which is no longer an option for them. So far, 30 people have taken advantage of this opportunity and taken courses in fields such as cosmetology, insurance, lock-smithing, jewelry-making, and photography.

Rabbi Rimon has also been fundamental in opening 25 new businesses started by former Gush Katif residents. "In Gush Katif," he explains, "there were about 200 businesses: supermarkets, a work tool manufacturer, a spice business, a bike shop, a shoe distributor, and more. What we've done is help some of these people get back on their feet."

One such business is Shirat Hayam, a date distributor. Another is a bicycle business. And another, a shoe distributor, is an inspiring illustration of how Rabbi Rimon makes things happen. "I met a man who was in a really terrible state," he recalls. "He had a huge supply of shoes and nowhere to sell them. I found a former Gush Katif farmer with a big truck. He transported the shoes to Allon Shvut, where we had a huge shoe sale. It was so successful that we made another one in Modiin."

"My goal," Rabbi Rimon explains, "is not *tzedakah* [charity]. It is really to help people who were once successful and independent start over again."

Rabbi Rimon has a vision for the future, including a proposal he made to a high-tech company that could provide a significant number of jobs. Currently, he is trying to raise seed money to finance this project, among others.

The Baltimore Connection

Two Baltimoreans – Rabbi Yigal Segal and his wife Rivky, formerly director of Rebbetzin Frieda K. Hirmes Women's Institute of Torah (WIT) – who made *aliya* last summer, have become active PR/fundraising volunteers for JobKatif. Rabbi Segal was interviewed recently about JobKatif on his brother's radio show (www.nachumsegal.com). Rivky is writing project proposals and helping Rabbi Rimon to organize fundraising trips abroad.

"We came on the day of the Disengagement," Rivky explains. "This was a very painful and difficult day to come into Israel. And we felt it the second that we landed. We felt it in the cab on the way to the hotel, and we felt it when we visited our friends.

"Political differences aside," she continues, "these people are in a tremendous amount of pain right now. This is not about being for or against Disengagement. This is about feeling concerned for fellow Jews who are very fine people and in great need right now."

On a recent visit to Nitzan, an area near Ashkelon where about 450 evacuees are now living, Rivky found a very bleak and depressing situation. "People are living in caravillas, temporary houses, one right next to the other," she explains. "They are here for the next two to three years, and then they are expected to move to a more permanent location. Most of these people are from Neve Dekalim and many are farmers. Because of their age, the government is pushing them to retire early.

"People who were once so busy with their lives have nothing to do. Many people I spoke to were very depressed. They didn't want to come out of their houses. They have very little energy. You still feel a sense of disbelief, like, did this really happen?

"One man I met showed me albums and albums of his life in Neve Dekalim. Beautiful pictures that he shared in pride. It was very sad."

Having said this, Rivky also saw glimmers of light. One man has retrained himself to work as a locksmith. "Another man I met, Ilan, a former restaurateur in Gush Katif, opened up a window in his caravilla, where he now sells ice cream and pizza. 'People want my store,' he told me. 'It gives them hope to see me succeeding.'"

This desire to see others succeed is also a reflection of the tremendous love for one's fellow that is felt in the community. Even when things are difficult, there is a sense of pulling together and supporting each other. In fact, Rivky recalls someone telling her that he'd do his shopping in Gush Katif even if prices were higher there. "I didn't look for bargains," he said. "It was important to me to feel that I was helping someone else to make a living."

Given the reality of the aftermath of those very difficult days last summer, what is most remarkable about Rabbi Rimon is his optimism. He doesn't criticize the government, or anyone for that matter. He is focused on doing what needs to be done. When I asked him how he remains so optimistic, he drew upon our sages' comparison of the Final Redemption with a deer.

"A deer goes down a mountain so that he can go up," he explained. "It looks like he is going down, but this is only so that he can go up. I believe that this is the beginning of something higher. God brought us to Israel, and it is not for nothing. I know that the situation is difficult, but I also know that this will take us to a higher level."

And We Know Not What To Do …
By Rabbi Yosef Elnekaveh

In a fascinating conversation that I had with former Sephardi Chief Rabbi Mordechai Eliyahu, Rabbi Eliyahu quoted the words of the Abudraham on the verse in the *tachanun* prayer, "And we know not what to do – but our eyes are upon You."

Rabbi Eliyahu said, "A Jew comes to pray. He enters the synagogue and kisses the *mezuzah*. And then he says, 'And I, through Your abundant kindness, come into Your house; I bow toward Your holy Sanctuary in honor of You.'

"Even when he is on his way to the synagogue, he says, 'I am going to the synagogue of our forefather Avraham to recite the morning service.'

"He takes his *tallit*, checks the four fringes, blesses them, and wraps himself within the *tallit*. Then, he takes his *tefillin*, puts them on his arm, tying the straps in the correct manner. Similarly, he puts the *tefillin* on his head in the appropriate way.

"The Jew sits down and prays. He reaches the part of the service where he recites the *korbanot*, closes his eyes, and concentrates upon the name of God. With much trepidation, he proclaims God as King, holding his *tzitzit* in his hand.

"He sits and sings the songs of praise to God, and then stands and says, 'And David blessed the Lord.' Then he gives charity, kisses his *tzitzit*, and sits down. He bows, kisses the *tefillin*, recites 'Holy, holy,' and then reaches *kriat shema*, during which he kisses his *tzitzit* again.

"Standing up once again, he recites the *amidah*, all of his limbs swaying, his entire essence and being at one with the prayer. He bows four times, takes three steps back in prayer, and waits.

"The *shliach tzibbur* starts to recite the prayer, and when he reaches *kedushah*, the Jew moves three steps forward and jumps slightly three times. Later, he bows again at *modim*.

"During *viduy*, he strikes his heart and lowers his head in the appropriate places, and cries out, 'Master of the Universe!'

"I came, I went in, I bowed, I stood, I sat, and stood again. I bowed, I kissed the *tefillin* and *tzitzit*, I stood again, bowed, jumped, struck my heart, lowered my head, and now, Master of the Universe, now that I have done all of that, what more can I do that I have not yet done?'"

While Rabbi Eliyahu was describing with great feeling all of the stages and expressions of prayer, I was thinking about the decades during which we lived in the Gaza Strip, which is located in the portion of Yehudah.

Dozens of families moved there, into temporary buildings, and gradually we built up a wonderful community based on kindness and Torah. We built and planted, and we observed all of the *mitzvot* associated with living in the Holy Land. We observed the laws of *shemittah* in the strictest manner, and we were careful regarding the restrictions against consuming any bugs in vegetables. We also scrupulously kept the laws pertaining to tithing our crops.

We established schools for Torah and general education, more than 20 *mikva'ot*, beautiful synagogues, study halls, and *Talmudei Torah*.

There were Torah publications and classes for our children, learning programs, colleges, rabbinical courts, and every other type of religious service.

And even when we suffered sniper fire, having stones and iron bars thrown at us, mortar raids, and every other type of hostile action from our enemies, we still remained faithful to our covenant with the Holy Land. And when the government started talking about uprooting our communities, we did whatever we could to prevent it. Lovingly, we increased our study of Torah. We opened our homes to visitors and set up groups to recite *Tehillim*. There were groups that studied the laws of *lashon hara*, groups for learning the *Zohar* and the Talmud, and such activities were constant and ongoing.

We held prayer services, supplications, gatherings, assemblies, and demonstrations. We went door to door, from house to house, a chain of fine Jews, stretching toward the Holy Temple.

We went out into the streets, into the cities. We held public and private fasts.

Our material and spiritual efforts knew no bounds. We appealed to the entire world, we gave charity, and put all of our thoughts into action.

And now, dear God,
We
Know not
What to do,
But our eyes are
Upon You...

The Spirit of Gush Katif: Don't Let It Get Washed Away
By Judy Lash Balint

www.jerusalemdiaries.com

November 23, 2005

It rained heavily this week all over Israel – not particularly notable for late November, unless you happen to be one of the 8,500 people who were evicted from their homes last August as part of the Gaza withdrawal plan.

For many of these Israelis, the heavy rains prove to be one more trial to endure in the turmoil that their lives have become since losing any semblance of normalcy more than three months ago.

At Ir HaEmunah (City of Faith), the tent city established by former residents of Atzmona in the wake of their eviction, parents desperately attempt to swoosh two to three inches of water away from the meager belongings in their makeshift homes. In between sweeps with a rubber floor sweeper, Moshe, 35, a father of six, explains that the rain seeped in during the early morning hours while everyone was still asleep on their iron cots. Anything left on the floor, including cardboard boxes of clothing and plywood bookshelves, is sopping wet and unlikely to dry out anytime soon. Someone had the foresight to build the communal toilets and showers on wooden planks, but kids who woke up to the sound of rain had to slosh through the water with damp towels to start their day.

"Welcome to the *ma'abarot* [temporary dwellings for Jewish refugees from Arab countries] of

2005," exclaims a middle-aged woman as she welcomes visitors to the mud-soaked entrance to Ir HaEmunah, just outside the southern town of Netivot.

"If you don't come to see it, you can't believe it," adds Michal, a former Atzmona schoolteacher. Michal explains that Atzmona residents had the opportunity to move to scattered apartments offered by the Disengagement Administration after the evictions. "But we know that ultimately we want to build a new community in the Negev together, and once we would be scattered it would be almost impossible to sustain that goal." So, the intrepid pioneers, who endured thousands of Kassam rockets and mortar attacks during their time in the far south of Gush Katif close to the terrorist nest of Rafiach, decided to take advantage of an offer of an empty industrial warehouse to set up their tent homes. More than 55 families are here, trying to negotiate a solution to their plight. The renowned Atzmona pre-army *mechina* program has relocated to the community of Yated, but the remaining residents try to maintain a positive attitude and routine amidst the difficult physical conditions. Just last week, a number of rundown caravans (mobile homes) were brought into the area, which are an improvement over the industrial tents shored up by plywood that make up the homes inside. One small, half-assembled playground sits starkly in the mud outside the caravans. Inside the cold, cavernous warehouse space, kids wander around, pushing at the water with their shoes.

Michal describes how they built the school rooms on the second floor of the structure in a three week period. But the school is not recognized by the state, so supplies are bought and salaries paid by the community itself. "We have lots of donations," Michal smiles. Michal and her friends are wearing the lavender fleece jackets provided by Project Warm-Up, an initiative operated and funded largely by Jerusalem-based English-speaking immigrants to provide warm winter coats for every evictee.

Until recently, none of the families had its own cooking facilities and meals were eaten communally, provided by a kibbutz catering service. Someone donated one electric hotplate burner for each family, "...and you can't imagine how good our first omelet tasted!" exclaimed Michal.

The inability to prepare meals for one's family is one of the most-often cited complaints of the evictees scattered in hotels all over the country. Parents don't go out to work (their previous workplaces vanished overnight), they don't shop and they don't cook. The kids of the hotel families don't help out – there's nothing for them to help with – so essentially all traditional family functions have been disrupted.

Michal says that the Ir HaEmunah people have now been told that it will be another two or three months until their new temporary homes in Lachish, south of Hebron, will be ready.

Meanwhile, the source of their strength, their synagogue, has been recreated by joining together two mobile homes. Residents managed to salvage their beautiful light wood synagogue seating and the Ark together with its blue velvet covering. "I cried when we *davened* there on the first Shabbat after we were evicted," says Michal. "But week by week, it's got better. We're resolved to rebuild ourselves," she adds.

A 40-minute drive past the turn-off to the Kissufim entryway to Gush Katif, brings us to the tiny community of Yavul, just a stone's throw from the border with Egypt. A drone hovers overhead monitoring the border crossings. Here at Yavul, dozens of pre-fab buildings sit in the muddy, sandy soil in varying states of completion. Pre-teen kids ride around on bikes and play in the sand. Inside the industrial-size tent that serves as meeting place, dining hall, and shelter from the rain, Drora Visner and Tzurit Yarchi describe their lives here. Yavul is now home to most of the evictees from Netzarim, which was one of the most dangerous places to live in Gush Katif. For years before the eviction, the IDF insisted that only bullet-proof vehicles could travel in and out. Today, the determined people of Netzarim are awaiting their permanent solution. Eighteen Netzarim families are in Ariel, almost three hours drive away. "We're looking forward to doing in the Negev what we accomplished in Gush Katif," Tzurit emphasizes. She explains that they hope to bring their experience, knowledge, and unique agricultural methods to build a new community. But most of all, "We want to preserve the spirit of Netzarim," she says. Drora nods in agreement, as she holds the hand of one of her 11 children, ages 2-23. Drora is a double-evictee. Her family was kicked out of Yamit when she was a child and re-established itself in Gush Katif. Her sister, Tiferet Trattner, was murdered by terrorists in Gush Katif in 2004.

Tzurit tells her visitors that the mourning over the Gaza withdrawal should be national. On the other hand, she adds, "While the state did a great crime here, we still have faith in the state. We just have to work to change the leaders."

Bryna Hilberg, one of the founders of the Gush Katif community of Netzer Chazani, now living in the guest house of Kibbutz Ein Tzurim, concurs. "The politicians made a mistake, but I still love my country," she emphasizes. Hilberg's family has paid dearly for their commitment. Their son Yochanan was killed in action while serving as an Israel Navy frogman. He was buried in the cemetery of Gush Katif. The Hilbergs were forced to exhume his body and rebury him when the Jews were forced out of Gush Katif. "I felt as if the state killed him again," she grimaces as she holds up a book dedicated to her son with his face adorning the cover. "It was the nightmare of my life," she recounts. Yochanan was reburied in Nitzan, close to the sea that he loved.

Bryna's husband was an expert in cultivating crops in the sand. Today, he's lucky to have a part-time job in the local grocery store.

Fellow Netzer Chazani evictee, Anita Tucker, tells visitors that while the loss of her physical community is painful, she and her neighbors feel that "it's the values, the spirit, the sense of community that couldn't be destroyed by the IDF bulldozers." Presently, half of the 60 families from Netzer Chazani are living in dormitories at the Chispin Yeshiva in the Golan, with the remainder at Ein Tzurim, not far from Ashkelon.

In a session of the Ministerial Disengagement Committee on November 23, Prime Minister Sharon said, "There is no doubt that building communities in the south is very important." Prime Minister's Office (PMO) Director-General Ilan Cohen added, "The vast majority of the residents will maintain their communal way of life."

Perhaps the Committee should make another visit to Nitzan, where remnants of several Gush Katif communities will be spending the next two years. The "caravillas" spread out in their neat rows over the former watermelon fields are now home to 320 families; eventually, when they're completed, some four or five months AFTER the evictions, 450 families will live here while they wait for permanent housing and employment solutions. It's hard to maintain a "communal way of life" when there's no store, massive unemployment, and little for the restless and traumatized teenagers to do. Here too, on this rainy day, residents are outside trying to deal with massive puddles and the mud that surrounds their homes. Containers sit outside some homes, in violation of the Disengagement Administration's directive. Most families couldn't squeeze the belongings from their former homes into the 90-sq./meter space they now inhabit. For the privilege of living in this neighborhood, the former Gush Katif residents pay $450 per month, which is deducted directly from their compensation packages.

Over at Kibbutz Chafetz Chayim, another religious kibbutz that has taken in Gush Katif evictees, Avraham Berrebi, formerly of Gadid, puts a brave face on his family's situation. Avraham, his wife Colette, and six children emigrated from France decades ago. "We fell in love with Gush Katif immediately," he recalls. Since the August evictions, the Berrebis have been shunted among Neve Ilan, Tiberias, and Chafetz Chayim. "We've become experts in moving," he chuckles. The only problem is that the Berrebis have no idea where their next move might take them when they have to leave Chafetz Chayim at the end of November.

Together with another 16 families from Gadid, they agreed to resettle in Massuot Yitzhak, not far from Ein Tzurim and Ashkelon. The Disengagement Administration has just informed them that they will make the necessary arrangements only for a minimum of 20 families. Exasperated, Berrebi explains that the other Gadid families got so fed up with waiting that they found other solutions.

If solutions aren't found quickly, there's a risk that the Zionist commitment, energy, and enterprise of the pioneers from Gush Katif will disappear with the rain.

Gaza's Best-Kept Secrets
By Michael Freund

Approximately 40 years ago, on the outskirts of Gaza City, a team of archeologists was busy conducting a dig not far from the sparkling blue waters of the Mediterranean Sea.

As they removed the layers of dirt and soil that had accumulated over the centuries, the excavators discovered what would prove to be one of the most remarkable finds in the Land of Israel: The remains of an ancient synagogue dating back some 1,500 years.

Needless to say, countless Jewish houses of worship from antiquity have been found throughout the length and breadth of the Holy Land. But what made Gaza's synagogue so unique is that it remains one of the largest, and oldest, ever found.

How about that for a little-known secret about Gaza?

Of course, nowadays the area is better known as the strip of land from which Prime Minister Ariel Sharon withdrew in August 2005, uprooting thousands of Israelis from their homes and paving the way for the rise of a Hamas-led Palestinian regime.

But Gaza has a rich and vibrant Jewish history to it, one that stretches back across the millennia, as the discovery of the ancient synagogue made clear. That history, however, was callously tossed aside when the Sharon government decided to pull out from the area.

In retrospect, the recklessness of that move has become all too apparent, as Gaza has been transformed into a launching pad for rocket attacks against the Jewish state, leaving southern towns and cities across the Negev, such as Sderot, in the crosshairs of Palestinian terrorists.

The fiasco of Israel's retreat has led many of those who supported the move to admit publicly the error of their ways. In November 2007, former Defense Minister Binyamin Ben-Eliezer of the Labor Party told an Israeli radio station, "I admit and I confess that I was among those who strongly supported Ariel Sharon [and the withdrawal]. Today I say, with my head held high, 'We erred, we made a very big mistake.'"

Other senior Israeli military officers, pundits, journalists, and politicians have likewise acknowledged that the Gaza pull-out has proven to be ill-advised. These include Brig.-Gen. (Res.) Moshe Ya'alon, the former IDF Chief of Staff; Maj.-Gen. (Res.) Giora Eiland, the former chairman of Israel's National Security Council; Maj.-Gen. Yair Naveh, the commander of the IDF's Central Command; and even Maj.-Gen. Gershon HaCohen, who served as the commanding officer in charge of the withdrawal.

But the effects of the pull-out were not limited to one part of the country or another. In fact, Israel's hasty retreat set the stage for its disastrous war in Lebanon in the summer of 2006. Don't believe me? Well, just ask Maj.-Gen. (Res.) Yiftach Ron-Tal, who served as commander of IDF ground forces at the time of the Gaza retreat.

In an interview with an Israeli newspaper in Otober 2006, here is what the General had to say: "In the year preceding the withdrawal, the army trained mostly for dismantling communities, and that prevented it from preparedness for the war in Lebanon. The training for the withdrawal not only prevented preparedness for such a war, but dragged it away from the consensus as a people's army. It is nearly certain that the excitement of those who led the decision and implementation of this is directly tied to the big failure in Lebanon."

Furthermore, added Gen. Ron-Tal, "I still cannot understand how Israel gave up parts of its land willingly and with abandon, and how the residents connected to that land were turned into criminals, instead of raising their dedication as a banner of preserving the Jewish identity of the State of Israel."

And neither, I might add, can many of us understand it.

Indeed, it is still hard to accept that the forcible removal of Gaza's Jews took place, or to believe that we could have possibly reached such a low point in the history of our nation.

After so many years of struggle and sacrifice, those once celebrated as pioneers by successive Israeli governments were demonized as obstacles to peace and treated with contempt by much of the Israeli media.

The Israel Defense Forces were deployed against the citizens of their own state, with the express purpose not of defending the Jewish people but of exiling them from parts of their ancestral patrimony.

And withdrawal under fire, once derided as capitulation to terror, suddenly became official government policy.

Israel's Left, of course, was gleeful, trumpeting the evacuation of Gaza as signaling the end of the dream of "Greater Israel."

But I believe they could not have been more mistaken.

For even in the face of uncertainty, the dream of return lives on. It might take years or even decades to achieve, but of one thing we can all be sure: The Jewish people will eventually bounce back, just as we have throughout history.

And soon enough, the sand dunes of Gaza will once again most assuredly be ours.

There are plenty of military and security reasons to justify Israeli rule over Gaza, if only because it serves as a gateway from the west to seize control over the entire country. Conquerors throughout the centuries, from Titus to Napoleon to the British, all entered Israel by way of Gaza, setting the stage for its eventual capture. Thus, to abandon Gaza and leave it in Palestinian hands is to ignore the key strategic role that the area has played throughout history.

More important, though, it ignores the fact that Gaza is an intrinsic part of the Land of Israel, the Jewish people's G-d-given patrimony.

In Hebrew, Gaza is referred to as "Aza," which means "strength" or "might." This might suggest the main quality that is needed in order for Israel to regain this strip of land, a quality that is sadly lacking among many of our current political leaders.

Or, perhaps, the message it conveys is somewhat deeper: that only if we muster within ourselves the strength to stand on faith in these most trying of times, will we merit to see G-d's promise, as contained in the Bible, quickly come to pass.

May this – one of Gaza's most precious of secrets – finally become revealed.

From Golden Stalks to Golden Grains and Back Again
By Shifra Shomron

This article appeared in Arutz Sheva, www.israelnationalnews.com.

July 23, 2007 (8 Av, 5767)

It's been a very long journey.

I stood outside the Nitzan caravilla site (trailer park) on a warm summer afternoon and watched the golden hay being baled. The heavy machinery ground loudly and spat out large, square, sweet-smelling bales. And as I stood silently and stared, I was once again a small five-year-old child with big brown eyes and short, curly brown hair, clutching my mother's hand tightly on a Shabbat afternoon in Chandler, Arizona.

After the Shabbat morning meal, my family would always go on a walk to Desert Breeze Park. And on the way there, when the season was right, we would stop and watch the hay being baled. My father would watch with a grin and a sparkle in his green eyes, explaining the hay baling process to us. My mother would be cheerfully amused, and my siblings and I would stare with wide-eyed wonder.

But time passed and, with God's help, my family made *aliyah* to Neve Dekalim, Israel. Agriculture was different there. Vast, rolling, gray hothouses took the place of open fields. Bug-free vegetables and beautiful flowers took the place of stalks of hay. Golden sand dunes and small communities replaced the urban sprawl. And only the summer heat remained the same.

I wasn't sorry for the change, nor was my family. We grew and blossomed in lovely Gush Katif.

But more time passed. Every paradise has to have its snake, and Gush Katif was invaded by several nasty vipers. The second intifada burst into being – roadside shootings, roadside bombs, attempted Arab infiltrations, mortars, Kassam rockets, Jews injured, Jews killed. Budding Jewish lives were cruelly snipped. And we learned to live under the shadow of Arab terror. We were hurting, and our wounds were raw and open and bleeding. But we persevered; we smiled bravely and dug our roots deeper into the sandy soil.

Then, the second viper showed its fangs. The Arabs were plucking our flowers when our Jewish government announced its desire to uproot us. The smile froze on our faces and our hearts were heavy. We set out to struggle. It was a long struggle and it was a brave struggle. There were demonstrations, a human chain, a Likud referendum in our favor, orange streamers, prayer vigils, street blocking, face-to-face campaigning, but the government won. And the Jewish nation lost. We were quickly uprooted, our houses were swiftly destroyed, and the Arabs smiled maliciously and paraded victoriously among the ruins.

Then, the people of Gush Katif were forced into two years of wandering. They traveled to Jerusalem. And from Jerusalem they dispersed to a great many locations, for their numbers were vast and the government did not know where to place them. And from Jerusalem they wandered as far south as Beersheva and as far north as the hills of the Galilee and the Golan. And eventually they settled in numerous, temporary caravilla sites. And they were sad, and they were weary, and they cried unto the Lord.

Slowly, slowly, they gathered strength. They recalled the five years of hardship they had borne in Gush Katif, and they remembered their fallen, and they remembered the joyful faces of their foes. And they refused to be beaten. If one listens, one can once again hear the determination in their voices and their visions for the future.

So, I stand and stare at the hay being baled outside the Nitzan caravilla site. It's a lovely day; the sun is shining, the sky is blue, and the golden hay is being gathered. And, for a bit, I allow myself the luxury of taking a trip along memory lane. My brown eyes smile and my hair blows in the wind. Despite the pre-fab trailer-homes, and despite the high unemployment, and despite the corrupt government and the national security problems, I laugh, enjoying a golden moment.

It's been a very long journey from the hay fields of Arizona to the hay fields of Nitzan, and we've been temporarily banned from paradise, but this little girl has grown up – with strong roots in the past and a fervent hope for the future.

The Service of the Heart
By Rabbi Yosef Elnekaveh

A person should serve his Creator every single day, at all times, everywhere, and in every situation. When a person knows what this service requires, he understands that he "should serve Him with all your heart." When he understands the meaning of the service of the heart, he becomes infused with the awareness and belief in the magnitude of his role in the world, and he will endeavor to fulfill it to the best of his ability.

The service of the heart is not precisely defined in the manner of other *mitzvot*, such as the ritual washing of the hands or putting on *tefillin*. This is because, as the author of *Chovot Halevavot* writes, these other commandments relate to the other limbs of the body. The service of the heart is, on the other hand, relevant to every situation in a person's life, whether we are walking, awake, or even asleep.

None of these obligations or duties contradicts the others. If anything, the opposite is true, and they complement each other. Putting on *tefillin* and separating *terumot* and *maaserot* (tithes) should be done wholeheartedly. Therefore, it could be said that the service and duties of the heart are included within the divine service of the other limbs.

The most unique duty in this category is the service of prayer, regarding which it is stated, "What is the service of the heart? It is prayer, about which the verse says, 'And you shall serve Him with all your heart.'"

This service is not time-bound, because it is carried out at all times, and it in fact transcends time. The person who was born to labor will see blessing from his toil, and his prayers reach the highest heavens. He creates a small opening with the words, verses, and chapters, and each word and letter illuminates, and the person realizes that this is the only type of service.

The service of prayer is the service of the heart, deep within which there are so many pearls. This is the innermost form of service, and it transcends everything.

There is regular prayer, and there are additional prayers. There are prayers with specific words, and then there are the words that are concealed among the extremities of our thought. These are the thoughts and feelings that bring tears to the eyes, and no words can truly convey their power.

All of the prayers that were recited this year were from the most sacred service of the heart. You saw the eyelashes of the child, the farmer who thought about the beautiful land that he had tended for the past 30 years that was about to be seized from him. And there was the grandmother wearing her kerchief, who wept inconsolably and could not be comforted.

This year was the year of prayer, the year of service – the service of the heart. …

Section Four:

Reports on Life After the Disengagement

Betrayal, Broken Hearts, and Pain Remain the Legacy of Ex-Gazans
By Toby Klein Greenwald

This article originally appeared in Cleveland Jewish News.

When I visited Debbie Rosen of Neve Dekalim, Gush Katif, at the Shalom Hotel in September, she said with sad eyes, "I'm looking forward to the day that I can bake my own challahs again."

The Rosens were among the 10,000 men, women, and children in Gush Katif, northern Gaza, and northern Samaria who were uprooted from their homes in mid-August. Debbie is baking challot in "her" kitchen again, this time in the Nitzan caravan camp. It's better than a hotel room, she says, but it's not the joyous occasion that challah-baking was before. When she moved in a few weeks ago, there were leaks and plaster all over the place. "It wasn't fit to live in," she says. Her exquisite garden in Gaza has been replaced by mud and flooded streets. Even the Chanukah holiday cannot wash away the sorrow. It brings back painful memories of what used to be.

"The worst part," she says, is that "almost everyone's forgotten us except for 'our' communities, the religious Zionists. Where are the left-wing non-religious who claim to care about humanitarian issues?" she asks. "And where is Ariel Sharon's efficient army? They knew how to pack up our belongings to get us out of Gush Katif. Why are the elderly from Gush Katif at the mercy of friends and volunteers to help them move their furniture out of containers, rebuild their closets, fix, and *shlep*? Some of these people are survivors of terror attacks and are disabled.

"When mortars were falling around us, the army said that it couldn't spare enough soldiers to solve the mortar problem. But when they decided to uproot us from our homes, there were tens of thousands and more than were sent to fight the Yom Kippur War. Doesn't the IDF have a maintenance division? Can none of them be spared now to help us put our homes, such as they are, back together again?"

A native Israeli who speaks perfect English, Debbie has been unemployed since the expulsion. The mother of six, ranging in age from 6-19, she had worked for the spokesman's office in Gush Katif, where she and her husband Shlomo lived for 20 years.

Reporters from Israel and abroad know Rosen as a walking encyclopedia on Jewish Gaza. Journalists still call her for information.

I first met Debbie more than two years ago, when she took a break from her hectic schedule to participate in a weekly creative writing class I gave to women in Gush Katif. One chill night in January 2003, I asked participants to "write about how you would feel the morning you're expelled from your homes."

They were shocked at the assignment, and some refused to write; others cried as they read their poems or essays. My goal had been to stretch their imaginations about something frightening. Ten days later, Ariel Sharon announced the Disengagement Plan, and the women were in shock.

"You should have told us to write about the coming of the Messiah," they said in anguish.

"We were told that we would be in the hotels for one week," says Debbie with barely controlled rage. That week stretched to four months for Rosen and her family. At the time of this writing, there are still between 200 and 300 families in hotels or tent camps.

Almost 2,000 people are still unemployed, even though in Gush Katif unemployment was virtually unknown, and the community even donated money and produce to the less fortunate. Rav Yosef Tzvi Rimon of Gush Etzion has created a grassroots effort and website (www.jobkatif.org.il) to help find jobs for people. He's had some success, but there is still a long way to go, and there is almost no help from the government.

People signed up for Ministry of Trade retraining courses in early September, but the courses have still not opened. One minister who had taken an interest in the evictees and tried to help was Matan Vilnai (Labor), but when he and the other Labor ministers resigned from Sharon's government, he lost his power base.

Chaim Altman, spokesman for the Disengagement Authority, told me in September that there are three types of housing for the Katif evicted: "immediate" (hotels and tent camps), "temporary" (caravan camps set up by the government), and "permanent" (real homes).

Only about 35 families from the northern Samarian communities of Ganim and Kadim have achieved the third category by using their compensation money to buy apartments in the Afula area or elsewhere. The other 1,900 families are still in either "immediate" or "temporary" dwellings. But the Disengagement Authority, apparently seeking a more favorable spin, has changed its terminology in the last few weeks, and now refers to the caravan camps as "permanent" housing.

Education is one of the Rosens' greatest worries. While they were in the Shalom Hotel in Jerusalem for four months, the children were sent to makeshift schools set up for the Gush Katif "refugees."

"My ten-year-old had five different teachers in the space of three months," says Debbie. "My six-year-old started first grade without the special 'first-day' events that we used to have in Gush Katif and that they have in most Israeli schools."

Now the youngster is in a Katif school, a bus ride away from Nitzan caravan camp, but even that is not without its problems. Parents have complained about the lack of vital equipment and about the paucity of psychological help, says Debbie. "There are also no bus shelters for the children, so they wait for their school buses in the pouring rain."

"The TV ads said, 'There is a solution for every settler,'" Debbie quotes bitterly. "We knew in advance it was a big lie, and now the whole country knows it, too, but no one does anything about it. The Prime Minister's office has revealed itself as the most inefficient organization in the State of Israel.

"Had we agreed to go to scattered rental apartments in failing towns throughout Israel," she adds, "it would be one more way to totally destroy our community life. It forces us to ask the question, 'Is that what the government wanted to happen?'"

Many people evicted from their homes in Gaza have still not received any compensation, including the first 50,000 shekels they were going to receive "the first few days after the Disengagement."

The Rosens filled out their paperwork for compensation in early September and haven't received any money yet.

What does the Disengagement Authority tell Debbie now when she asks where her compensation is?

"They say, 'It's on the way.'"

Regarding their current conditions, Debbie says, "My friend describes Nitzan (caravan camp) as a Hollywood set. They built the scenery, but they know it will be destroyed, so they didn't put a lot of effort into it. There is no soccer field or basketball court, no youth clubhouse. Many youth are still in distress."

A few weeks ago, a few pizzerias were opened, but there is no shopping area. The only businesses that have reopened are cottage industries – such as a cosmetologist or a seller of paper goods – operating out of their homes.

The evicted are still paying their mortgages, and people who rented privately are being singled out from those who rented from government bodies or owned land.

The agriculturists have their own set of crises. For example, Assaf Asis, whom Jewish organizations and the Israeli government like to hold up as their "poster boy" because he spoke to the Disengagement Authority well in advance of the Disengagement, has still not received a single penny in compensation for his successful geranium-export business, which he transplanted to southern Ashkelon. He is more than three million shekels in debt now because he is honoring his European contracts in spite of the government's foot-dragging.

Kassam rockets fall almost daily on Ashkelon now, not too far from Asis's greenhouses. They are fired by Palestinian terrorists operating out of the area of the former Jewish community of Dugit, which was destroyed by the Disengagement forces.

Forgotten Refugees
By Rachel Ginsberg

*This article originally appeared in
Mishpacha Magazine.*

It was the omelet that made Tzipporah Haddad realize just how much her family missed a home-cooked meal.

When they were thrown out of their homes with the destruction of the Gush Katif communities, the Haddads and their eight children couldn't imagine that they would be living out of suitcases for the next nine months, along with hundreds of families stranded in hotels, youth hostels, vacation villages, and tent cities. First squashed into a room at the Jerusalem Hyatt Hotel and then transferred to a military vacation village, the Haddads finally unpacked nine months later in their own pre-fab "caravilla" in the evacuee enclave of Nitzan, off the Ashdod-Ashkelon highway.

"The first night in Nitzan, as we were all exhausted from the move, some caring neighbors who had also just moved in shared their supplies with us – a bottle of oil and some eggs," relates Tzipporah. "There was still no stove, but I had a small electric burner. So, unearthing a frying pan, amidst the boxes, I started scrambling the eggs. All the children stood around as if I were preparing a *korban* [offering], reverent silence with tears in their eyes. You see, it was the first meal their mother had prepared for them since the day of the expulsion."

Dwelling on the destruction of her home is so mind-boggling, says Tzipporah, that she prefers to focus on gratitude instead. At least her family has had a proper roof over their heads. Evacuees from Atzmona spent the winter of 2005 in the tent city they pitched on the outskirts of Netivot called Ir HaEmunah (City of Faith). Many of the expulsion victims of Elei Sinai are living in Ohalei Sinai, a tent park set up on a lot outside Kibbutz Yad Mordechai close to the northern Gaza border. And her husband, an accountant, works in nearby Ashkelon. Of the 2,200 people who lost their jobs in the Disengagement's aftermath, 80% are still unemployed.

She also tries not to dwell on the fact that most of the family's worldly possessions, including all the *sifrei kodesh*, were either damaged or destroyed when the storage depot they were using flooded due to the heavy winter rains. Personal belongings of many expelled families are still stored away in sealed containers at the Kastina Junction in the Negev, if the contents haven't been either looted by roaming Bedouin or permanently damaged by the heat, which reaches 160 degrees inside the steel crates under the baking Negev sun. Many containers have remained untouched by their owners, following a government ruling that families may access their containers only when they are moved to their permanent site. Families that did open their containers have filed complaints for damaged or stolen property. Refrigerator doors melted from the heat; other major appliances were damaged beyond repair. One family that moved into a caravilla before Pesach found all the furniture shredded by rats.

Yisrael Lilienthal, 72, considers himself fortunate. After several months at the Kastina Junction, his four containers were set down in the back of his caravilla in Nitzan. The contents of two fit into the house. The other two, giant red metal shipping crates, are still sitting in the yard, in lieu of a storage shed, for the price of 14,000 shekels, paid to the Disengagement administration. The casualties were anything made with glass, porcelain, or formica. The furniture was in pretty good shape.

Days before the Disengagement, families didn't know if they should pack or not. Most people didn't really believe such a thing could actually happen. There would be some miracle at the last minute. But Wednesday morning, the official expulsion date, Rav Mordechai Eliyahu sent a message to the people of Gush Katif: "The decree has been decreed," and he encouraged people to salvage what they could. The Lilienthals had a staff of volunteers to help them – dozens of yeshiva boys who camped out in their home all summer.

Two sons who lived nearby, one from Atzmona with nine children and one from Kfar Darom with eight, said not to pack. "But I'm a little older, maybe a little more practical, maybe a little more nervous."

All that remains of their 260 sq. meter villa in Neve Dekalim are the photographs – the magazine kitchen, the dining room where dozens of yeshiva students from Jerusalem would converge every Shabbat, the sculpted lawn. The Lilienthals were escorted away from their home by a cadre of army personnel, but were allowed to come back twice the following week to pack before Neve Dekalim was bulldozed over.

"We left Wednesday night. We spent Thursday in front of the television watching them drag the rest of my family away," says Brooklyn-born Esther Lilienthal. "We saw our son Elitzur, a Rabbi and Torah scholar who can barely walk, being hauled away from the shul in Kfar Darom." Rabbi Elitzur, who joined his family during the expulsion, was injured in a terrorist ambush several years ago while driving from his home in Samaria to a pre-dawn Kabbalah *shiur* together with Rabbi Elimelech Shapiro. Rabbi Shapiro was killed on the spot.

Families that were stuck in hotels for months received eviction notices the week before Pesach. They were to be moved to two caravilla sites that are still in the process of being built – Amatzia, in the Lachish region, and Kibbutz Ein Tzurim – plus newly erected caravans in Nitzan. Some of the new houses didn't have plumbing installed yet; others were still missing doors and windows. Osnat Miness, who was stuck in the military vacation camp in Ashkelon, had given birth the week before to her 13th child; her sister's family was evicted from the Jerusalem Hyatt but discovered their new home in Ein Tzurim was still uninhabitable. The entire clan camped out in their mother's Tel Aviv living room over Pesach. The new caravilla sites are pretty much in the middle of nowhere, and children who finally settled in schools will again have to reacclimate. Furthermore, these homes are also only temporary. The leases are for just two years. After that, the government has promised to reunite the Gush Katif communities in permanent housing in planned towns in the sparsely populated Lachish and Negev regions.

Although this year's exodus from Egypt was an eviction from a Jerusalem hotel to an unfinished caravilla in Ein Tzurim, Dana Zelinger prefers to look toward the future. Some families, she notes, are still stranded in hotels.

"The hardest thing for us mothers was the supervision," says Dana, mother of seven whose youngest is five. "These are the first weeks in almost a year that we're sleeping in a home as a family. In the hotels, the parents and children are separated by a public hallway and a locked door. What if a child wakes up in the middle of the night? I had no idea what time my older kids went to sleep, or if they were even in their rooms or perhaps wandering around downtown Jerusalem at midnight. It's been a real challenge to get back to our family unit."

The Zelingers, from Neve Dekalim, spent seven months in the Jerusalem Gold Hotel adjacent to the Central Bus Station, where she served as activities coordinator for the refugees.

"There, every minute has to be organized. In a normal home, your child comes home after school, flops down on the couch, takes a snack from the kitchen, and 'just is.' In the hotel, there is no 'just.' He can't hang out in the lobby, and he can't shoot hoops in the bus station.

"People assume that after almost a year, we've all gotten our lives back together, we've picked up our compensation checks and gone forward," Dana says. "It's not true. Almost no one has received full compensation. Unemployment is rampant and savings are gone. No permanent housing solutions have been created yet."

When the Zelingers arrived at the Disengagement Office (SELA) to pick up the keys to their caravilla, they were shocked to discover that SELA had prepared a contract for them, stating that the lease was only for a year and a half and that they wanted the rental money, $450/month for 18 months, up front. They additionally demanded another security check for NIS 16,000 for the kibbutz. According to the Compensation Law, evacuees are entitled to two years rent-free, but other families say they have been told that the first two years of housing at $450/month will be deducted from their compensation package, if they ever receive it.

In Neve Dekalim, Tzvi Zelinger worked as an electrician, and Dana ran a popular stationery store, the regional center for gifts and school supplies. "The compensation we were told we'd receive for the store just about covers the liquidation expenses. Anyway, it's all theoretical because so far we haven't seen a shekel of it. We'll probably have to go to court. In truth, I don't believe the government has the money to cover their compensation promises. They spent the entire Disengagement budget training soldiers and destroying the region. Now there's nothing left for us, the victims of the expulsion."

Each expelled family has received an initial NIS 50,000, which was intended to be used to get them back on their feet. But as savings become depleted and most former breadwinners are unemployed or in retraining programs, much of that money is already gone. This advance alone has already cost the government close to $20 million. Families are skeptical that, even with any goodwill, the state budget would never be able to meet the level of equitable compensation.

Dana says her most heartbreaking task at the hotel was working with the forced pensioners, productive men over 50 who had no plans of retiring for the next ten years, whose careers were bulldozed together with their homes and now, at their age, find it impossible to start over. "For them, the hotel, the limbo, is torture. Some have tried to start new businesses, others have been brave enough to try retraining. But the farmers, the store owners, the civil servants, how do you start over at 55?"

One of these men is Moshe Shalva, 54. With his long bushy beard, tucked-out flannel shirt, and flying *tzitzit* underneath, he's out of place in the subdued elegance of a hotel lobby. It's easier to picture him being whipped by the ocean winds coming off the Katif sand dunes. For 23 years, Shalva ran a successful Judaica business in Neve Dekalim. He's still waiting for compensation for both his home and business. The NIS 50,000 advance is being depleted by daily expenses to sustain his large family – that is, whatever funds are left after the mortgage payments on his destroyed home are deducted every month.

One of the ironies of the compensation package is that to get the initial NIS 50,000, a special government-controlled account had to be opened. Bank Tefahot, Israel's largest mortgage bank, was about to sue the government for the millions of dollars it would lose on defaulted mortgage payments for homes that would no longer exist, until the Treasury determined that the banks would still receive their mortgage payments – from the evacuees' compensation accounts.

The Shalvas have four generations in the hotel. Moshe's mother, 92 and clear as a whistle, is the oldest Gush Katif evacuee, having lived with her son in Neve Dekalim for 17 years since her husband died. She was determined to stay to the end, but was taken out of the area a week earlier by her children. They didn't want her, a Holocaust survivor, dragged out by soldiers. Moshe, father of 12, also has married children and grandchildren in the hotel. The Shalvas have younger children too, including a little girl with Downs Syndrome.

The Shalvas' evacuation history is bizzare. They were the last family carried out of Yamit ("each soldier took one limb") in 1982, following the Camp David Accords, when they were put on a bus and dropped off at the bus station in Beersheva. From there, with four children under four, they made their way to the fledgeling community of Neve Dekalim in Gush Katif. And again, they were the very last family evacuated from the region, most of which was cleared out on Wednesday, August 17. The Shalvas managed to stay in their home until the following Tuesday, witnessing the desecration and pillaging of their once pastoral, verdant city.

"Don't think we came out shooting," Moshe Shalva recalls. "It was really quite strange and anticlimactic. Each time the eviction forces showed up, we had another excuse. We agreed that we would all leave together, but on August 17, my wife was in the hospital with my special-needs daughter. She didn't return until Shabbat. On Sunday, another daughter fainted. In the end, it was already Tuesday, but by then the evacuation forces had already left to dismantle the northern Shomron settlements and only the guards were left, so there was actually no one to evict us. The one remaining officer told me, 'I'll put a bus and an ambulance outside your home, but I won't move a Jew out of Eretz Yisrael.' We were in a real pickle. All around us was destruction. Was there really anything to stay for? I was ready to leave, but my kids wouldn't budge. Stalemate. In the end the Rabbinic leadership intervened and convinced the kids to leave. On the way out, we stopped at all the towns that had already been turned to rubble, tore our clothes, and recited the blessing, *Baruch Dayan Emet* [Blessed is the true Judge]."

Was it hard to look?

"It's indescribable. I don't ever want to have to see such a thing again."

The public buildings in Neve Dekalim were left intact, handed over to the Palestinian Authority. Moshe Shalva's Jewish bookstore is now part of the campus of the Islamic College. So far he hasn't seen any compensation for the business, although he signed an agreement that would entitle him to two and a half years of his last average income. In the meantime, he's trying his hand at various ventures, but nothing seems to go. "At my age," he says, "it's too late to start over."

"Too late to start over" is the distressing slogan for about 80% of the unemployed residents of Nitzan, an evacuee enclave of close to 500 families, ten minutes from Ashkelon, comprising rows and rows of red-roofed caravans standing on what last year was still a watermelon field. The government, hoping the red roofs and elegant name would make them more palatable for families whose own magnificent homes were destroyed, rushed to put up hundreds of these "caravillas," paying contractors $90,000 per caravan – about four times what similar structures are worth on the open market.

In Nitzan, the caravillas range in size from 60 sq. meters to 90 sq. meters (1,000 sq. ft.) for larger families, the walls are paper-thin, there are only shower stalls and no bathtubs (mothers bathe their small children in laundry basins), kids hang around in the afternoons with nothing to do, and most neighbors are unemployed, struggling with the $450/month rent to be deducted from their compensation. Over 100 food packages are delivered to Nitzan every Friday for families that can no longer afford basic staples or chickens for Shabbat. Some have resorted to begging. On Jerusalem's Ben Yehudah pedestrian mall, a middle-aged man in a business suit is in charge of a daily charity collection.

Chaya Rabinovitch heads a privately-funded team of ten social workers to deal with families in crisis in the Disengagement's aftermath. A resident of the hilltop outpost Achiya in Samaria, she travels over an hour each way to Nitzan daily, trying to help families put their lives back together. She, her husband, and their 11 children picked up and spent the better part of last year in Neve Dekalim, where she worked for the Department of Social Services.

"Dozens, if not hundreds, of families are on the verge of collapse, both financially and emotionally," she states. "The men, dejected and hopeless, don't even go out. They just stay home and watch television. It's tragic to see how successful individuals have been reduced to indigent, idle dependants.

"The government really goofed when they set up the apparatus for post-expulsion social services. First, they assumed that only one out of ten families would need some sort of help. They didn't take into account that every family suffered a major, life-shaking trauma. Then, seeing they were understaffed, they sent young, inexperienced social workers who were on the other side of the political fence, who had no idea how to deal with such complex issues that the families were dealing with, such as removal from their homes, financial ruin, and intense feelings of betrayal."

Although the government has allocated an additional $2 million to be spent on social services for the evacuees in the coming year, Rabinovitch is skeptical about its effectiveness. "There is a very basic lack of trust regarding any government overtures, and families just don't feel the social workers are really on their team. Just recently one Social Services employee who is working with the youth told one teenager, 'We'll help you forget what you went through.' The boy was horrified. 'You've taken away my home, and now you want to take away my memories?!'

"The youth, who are thought to be the most resilient, are in fact in a very fragile state right now," Rabinovitch explains of the 1,200 youths aged 12-18. "Many of them are dealing with the effects of terror over the last five years, of friends who died, of what they consider betrayal of their country and the destruction of the only home they knew. And after all that, there is tremendous anger at their parents and at their community leaders, who they believe should have put up a stronger fight instead of just passive resistance. There have been cases of breakdowns, and even suicide attempts. But even with the 'normal, healthy' kids, in school – if they actually show up in school – many have become floaters, have lost their ability to concentrate, and have exhibited inability to stick to tasks. The saddest are those who have gone to the army, university, or yeshiva or high school dorms. In addition to their other problems, they don't even have a place to go home to."

Michal Shomron of Neve Dekalim/Jerusalem Gold/Ein Tzurim manages a fund to help the 250 evacuee college students, most of whom found their financial support and tuition base disappear when their parents' finances collapsed. Scattered among campuses across the country, some don't even have bus fare to return "home" to visit their families wherever they may temporarily be living.

At Ir HaEmunah, the tent city built on an abandoned factory lot outside Netivot in the Negev, these former Gush Katif residents prefer to look toward the future instead of feeling betrayed by the past. Most of Ir HaEmunah is comprised of expatriates of the Gush Katif town of Atzmona, and many of those families were first evacuated 24 years ago from the Sinai settlements. Now they are being evacuated for the third time, but this time they are going willingly – to Kibbutz Shomriya in the sparse Lachish region, where the government has given them housing from the failing kibbutz to build their new community. Each kibbutz family was paid $300,000 in cash to resettle somewhere else – a sum any expelled family has yet to receive. The residents of Atzmona refused to be scattered in hotels around the country, choosing instead to hold onto their community under their own auspices at all costs, even if it meant living in tents and rickety caravans through the last harsh winter months. They packed their own containers so they know where their possessions are, and they set up an independent school system, yeshiva high school, and various community services without relying on government assistance or compensation, most of which hasn't yet come through anyway.

Zevulun Kalfa, Ir HaEmunah's "mayor," says that a Jew can dwell in darkness, "but we have chosen the light. We will once again rise from our shattered lives and once again make the desert bloom. It will be a different desert but it's all Eretz Yisrael. And we're coming to the finish line with our community intact, our future goals clear before us."

Most evacuees, those scattered in hotels and other temporary arrangements, haven't yet seen the light at the end of the tunnel, but Kalfa explains that a Jew has to look at the best side of his situation, however difficult. "It's true that the situation is awful, that destroying people's homes and livelihood is horrific, but there are many things that are bigger than me that I can't yet understand. I look at what it was like decades ago, when we had no country at all, and from that reference point I look toward the future."

Compensation is being delayed for many families because they just don't have the proof of residency the government demands.

"Try to prove you've lived in a town for 27 years, when electricity and phone bills are only stored seven years back in their computer systems," comments Rachel Saperstein, who moved to Nitzan after several months at the Jerusalem Gold. "The Interior Ministry has a detailed file on every one of us. They don't need our children's report cards to prove our residency. It's pure harassment. Can you think of more insidious harassment than demanding families do DNA testing to prove parenthood? Of course, no one agreed to that. They are trying to make our lives as difficult as possible, to send out a message that this is what's going to happen to everyone who doesn't cooperate with future expulsions – remember, Olmert is talking about another 80,000 people in the next four years."

The Sapersteins moved from New York to Jerusalem 38 years ago, and made the move to Neve

Dekalim in 1997. Rachel Saperstein has been an English Second Language instructor for 30 years, and wrote textbooks that are used in Israeli high schools. Moshe, a former *Jerusalem Post* columnist, one-time nature reserve warden, and avid blogger, lost an arm and an eye in the Yom Kippur War, and lost another two fingers on his "good" hand when his car was shot up in a terrorist ambush in Gush Katif in 2002. Ahuva Amergi, the woman in the car in front, was killed.

After their daughter was almost killed by a bomb on a bus in 1995, the Sapersteins sold their Jerusalem apartment, divided the funds among their struggling married children, and moved south. They fell in love with Gush Katif, "the most beautiful part of the country. We took a dilapidated shack and turned it into a magnificent villa."

The Sapersteins are not eligible for home compensation, due to a clause in the Compensation Law revoking eligibility for those who rented on the private market, those who initially rented publicly and then switched to private housing, and those, like the Sapersteins, who rented from the municipality even though the housing was originally government public housing.

But Moshe Saperstein says he considers himself one of the lucky ones. As a disabled war veteran he receives a monthly government pension, while friends and neighbors who were farmers lost their livelihood and are on the edge of destitution.

"For the last five years we lived under bombardment – rockets, mortars, shootings – but we didn't run away. We believed in holding onto our land. I would still prefer to live like that than to being thrown out of my home. A thriving, productive people have been turned into depressed refugees. We've seen the disintegration of a community and the humiliation of its citizens. This I will not forgive. To watch our shul being razed to the ground, with Arab terrorists dancing in the background. I have never seen the footage. I will not look at it."

But Mrs. Saperstein, 65, is not one to sit around and feel sorry for herself as a refugee. She has turned her caravilla into a charming home, with every room reflecting her artistic flair. "This place could have been a horror," she says, "but don't let my flower pots and throw rugs deceive you. I made a 'home sweet home' for me and my husband, but this place is nothing more than a refugee camp."

From her cluttered hotel room, she started the Band-Aid Fund, now called Operation Dignity, distributing a white envelope of NIS 500 to each displaced family. She has made four such distributions so far, making especially sure families not living off hotel food get their envelopes. "For some families, this is literally bread-and-butter money," she says.

The Sapersteins decided to throw in their lot with the Nitzan residents "because we feel we need to be together with our community," says Mrs. Saperstein. "We work with the information service, and feel we have to continue this. It's important to live with others who went through what we did – the bombardments, the expulsion. Who else can understand us? Anyway, this is also only temporary. Within five years the whole community will be moving to the Lachish region where we hope to build a beautiful town. It will never be Gush Katif, but I believe in looking toward the future. By then I'll be 70. I'm looking forward to the challenge."

Confirming what former Gush Katif residents and their advocates already knew, State Comptroller Justice Micha Lindenstrauss recently gave the government failing grades for its handling of the 1,750 families evicted from their homes in Gaza last summer. Lindenstrauss writes, "The State and its institutions failed in their treatment of the expelled citizens of Gush Katif. We are aware of the fact that the bodies that were established for the evacuation and absorption of the residents had to work in non-routine conditions, but this report shows that there were grave mistakes in their preparation, which caused harm to the evacuees and caused them unnecessary and very painful suffering. It is obligatory to investigate in depth the failures described herein."

Lindenstrauss slammed the Disengagement Administration (SELA) for not preparing adequate immediate temporary housing for the days following the withdrawal and longer-term temporary housing for the period until permanent housing is completed. SELA prepared only seven temporary housing centers, when in fact 31 were necessary. Hotels and campuses were to be used for a maximum of seven to ten days, but up to Pesach, hundreds of families had yet to be resettled.

Criticism was also leveled at the treatment of the evacuees' property. The report notes that hundreds of families were cut off from their properties for many months, and that many complaints of damaged or stolen property have still not been addressed because of unresolved disputes between SELA and the Defense Ministry.

However, Justice Lindenstrauss also admonished the residents for not cooperating with the government before the expulsion date. But at a Knesset Audit Committee hearing on the comptroller's report, former Gaza Coast Regional Director Avner Shimoni defended the residents' position. "I have no obligation to cooperate with those who come to throw me out of my home. On the other hand, just like the government knew how to bring in thousands of policemen and soldiers to deport us, they also should have been ready for us on that date, and they weren't."

"Even if I had tried, I wouldn't have been able to think up a harsher or more brutal way to carry out the Disengagement, to expel the residents of Gush Katif," Shlomo Wasserteil told a Knesset committee convened to evaluate the consequences of the Disengagement. Wasserteil, a founder of the once-thriving community of Ganei Tal, built the largest geranium nursery in the Middle East, supplying plants all over Israel and eventually breaking into the European market. "There are many big examples, but here's a small example," Wasserteil told the MKs. "The first bus that was supposed to take the expellees to their new homes stopped in the middle of the way because the driver's permit expired. He let the children off in the middle of the road, in the middle of nowhere, at 12:30 a.m. The children slept on the sidewalk."

Wasserteil recounted how there was little advance planning, how a high-school dorm was given a half-hour notice that a busload of shell-shocked expellees would be arriving for an indefinite stay, how hotels weren't given advance notice of the refugees' arrival, and how on the first night the deportees were shuttled from one hotel to another because there were no signed government agreements.

Despite the hardships and hurdles, one industry that has persevered, at least domestically, is Gush Katif's famous bug-free vegetable enterprise. Its two friendly competitors, Chasalat and Glatt Alim, have succeeded in continuing to provide nearly 100% of the Israeli market demand for bug-free lettuce. Yaakov Reicher, Glatt Alim's marketing manager, says it hasn't been easy. Some middle-aged farmers felt they just didn't have the energy to reestablish themselves somewhere else. Furthermore, compensation is still being processed. Yet even as the company has not yet seen a shekel from the governement, it rented land privately in the southern Negev and took private investments to reestablish its industry. The domestic side is almost to capacity, but at this point the overseas market has not yet reflourished.

Farmers in Gush Katif were considered among Israel's most successful. Their annual exports totalled $100 million, or 15% of Israel's agricultural exports. Gush Katif exported to Europe 95% of Israel's bug-free lettuce and greens, and 70% of its organic vegetables. The Jews of Gush Katif operated 3,600 dunams (890 acres) of hot-houses before the withdrawal. Later, with international assistance, the Palestinian Authority was able to reactivate three-quarters of them, even though initially much of the equipment and structures were destroyed or damaged by raiding Arabs. Yet the Gaza Arabs who have taken over the hot-houses reported to the Israel-PA Coordination Office that they have failed in growing bug-free vegetables. They had hoped to build on the region's previous success and cash in on the market the Israelis had built up over the years, but the blessings of the land that fell on Gush Katif's Jews were not to fall on them.

Israeli Teen Refugees Attempt Suicide, Drop Out
By Aaron Klein

This article appeared in WorldNetDaily.com.

July 6, 2006

Jewish teenagers evacuated by Israel last summer from the Gaza Strip experience high rates of suicide attempts and eating disorders, drop out of school, and abuse drugs and alcohol in large numbers, according to a report presented to the Knesset yesterday.

The report also listed an increased risk of heart attacks and emotional distress among adults evacuated from Gush Katif, the former Jewish communities of Gaza. The majority of refugees are unemployed, have yet to find permanent housing, and have not received the full compensation promised to them by the Israeli government.

"The situation is extremely grave," said Dror Vanunu, a former Gaza resident and the international coordinator for the Gush Katif Committee, a major charity organization representing the Gaza Jewish refugees. "It is at emergency status in many cases."

The Forum for Israel, a nonprofit group also working with Gush Katif refugees, outlined for the Knesset major problems facing evacuated families.

The Forum reported a rise in suicide attempts among Gush Katif teenagers since the evacuation last August and pointed to an elevation in suicidal thoughts and eating disorders. The report also said 30% of former Gush Katif teenagers either failed to integrate in new schools or failed their final exams.

Social workers said the teenagers have been finding it difficult to develop relationships and have been increasingly abusing alcohol and drugs. Some have been admitted to psychiatric hospitals.

Among adults, the Forum linked newly formed cases of heart disease to the distress caused by the evacuation.

In August, Israel evacuated its nearly 10,000 Jewish citizens from Gaza. Successive Israeli governments over the years had urged thousands of Israelis to move to Gaza and build communities there. Israel pledged compensation packages and aid to the expelled residents.

Prior to the Gaza evacuation, the vast majority of Gush Katif residents lived in large homes in landscaped communities. Many were farmers, tending to the area's famous technologically advanced greenhouses that supplied Israel with much of its produce. The Gush Katif unemployment rate was less than 1%.

But the Gush Katif groups and Israel's own Disengagement Administration report 51% of Gaza's Jewish refugees are unemployed, and only 21% of former Gush Katif businesses have re-opened. The Disengagement Authority was tasked with compensating the Gaza refugees.

The Israeli government stated it would provide temporary housing solutions for all expelled Gush Katif residents. But 200 of the approximately 1,750 former Gush Katif families are living in university dormitories, motels, and guesthouses. Most families now reside in the Israeli Negev desert in small, government-built, prefabricated "trailer villas." Residents there live mostly in crowded conditions, in many cases lacking enough bedroom space to accommodate their families.

"You can punch through my wall," a resident of Nitzan, the largest Gush Katif trailer community, told WND. "My friends come to visit me in coffee shops because there is not enough room in my living room for them to be comfortable."

Of Nitzan residents, 70% are unemployed.

Residents of the Negev trailer camps are mostly former farmers, many of whom now say they are not sure what they will do.

"The land is much different here than what Gush Katif farmers are used to," explained Anita Tucker, one of the pioneer farmers of Katif. "Most of the techniques used in the greenhouses in Gaza were specific to the land and environment. Now farmers will have to develop new ways for these new lands and the different kind of soil."

According to the most recent Gush Katif status report, many of the Jewish children expelled from Gaza suffer from a full range of traumatic and post-traumatic stress symptoms, yet many refugee sites lack youth counselors and activity centers. Budgets for youth programs expired in March.

Thirty Years in Thirty Minutes
By Anita Tucker

Constructing a community, a public building, or a home all demand defining goals, identifying a location, planning, permits, financial backing, and building, and then planning and filling the structures with functional and aesthetic furnishings. Most important and most difficult is filling it with people, content, meaning, and then evaluating its success in meeting the original goals.

It is a big team effort that can take years. Destroying it all takes only minutes.

I lived in Netzer Chazani for 30 years. We built this town on bare sand dunes that were not inhabited since the time of Avraham and Yitzchak, our forefathers, who lived there. We built from scratch – synagogues, *mikva'ot*, schools, community centers, youth centers, homes, businesses, playgrounds, sports fields, swimming pools, agribusinesses, community-based concerns, and light industry.

Most important and challenging, we succeeded in filling them all with meaningful contents.

These communities became known as Gush Katif.

When it was decided by the Knesset of Israel that bulldozers would destroy it all, piles of rubble remained of this flourishing community.

Soon the shifting winds of the renewed desert-like area again covered the rubble with sand. This once blossoming oasis is again empty sand dunes as it was after our Patriarchs moved.

We were careful to take out with us the Torah scrolls and the pictures and writings of our rabbi, the renowned scholar Rabbi Yitzchak Arama, murdered by Arab terrorists two years prior.

Our youth carried out the heavy Torah scrolls that sat safely in the sanctuary, read and reread year after year, generation after generation.

Many of the scrolls were covered by the traditional Sephardic wood and metal coverings, our youth hugging them with great love, aware that this was what they still had left of the town where they were born, grew up, and had hoped to live.

The traditions, the spirit, the learning, and the vision that are the contents of those beloved Torah scrolls hugged and protected our families as they left Gush Katif. We struggled to look forward, yet we could not easily forget the pain of destruction.

The families wandered from tents to hotel rooms to interim caravan-type living quarters, struggling for survival as humans, as families, as communities, as Jews at home in the State of Israel, as soldiers in our Israel Defense Forces.

All this interim period, we were, as well, dealing with the drawn-out bureaucratic procedure and negotiations to try and receive appropriate compensation for our businesses and homes. This has been a very trying and frustrating challenge, and in most cases it is not yet near completion as appeals are yet in procedure.

The communities were spread out in every direction. However, each community made superhuman efforts to keep together. Our community leadership wisely utilized those eternal values and spirit carried out of Gush Katif to give strength to the community. The community in turn gave strength to the families, and the families to their members.

With the eternal Torah values and spirit keeping the community together, we hoped and expected to build anew as a community as defined by the Disengagement-Compensation Law.

Two-and-a-half years later, having easily defined our goals, we suddenly discovered how much more difficult it would be to identify locations, to plan, to apply for approvals, etc. However, my community has accomplished this in cooperation with the government ministries.

We now seek to define our financial backing, which, not by chance, connects with our long-term goals.

For my town, Netzer Chazani, the first town built in Gush Katif in 1976, we will be receiving a government budget for building anew and we will invest all our compensation, plus additional loans, in building anew.

Yet we still can't begin construction in lieu of destruction as we had so hoped!

According to the latest adjusted government figures required for payment prior to signing the contract, there are still some gaps in the financing.

Our experiences have taught us to seek the solution in the challenge.

Our big challenge today in building a new town in Israel is how to connect to *Am Yisrael*, the People of Israel.

There was a terrible lack of dialogue, a lack of identification, a lack of brotherhood among Jews of different thinking and background during and after the Disengagement from Gush Katif, Gaza.

The position of Jewry around the world and the position of Jewry in Israel point to a screaming need for dialogue and rallying around the eternal Jewish values of those Torah scrolls that our youth hugged as they carried them out of the ruins of our communities.

Our beloved Jerusalem, more than ever, prays to us for unity around these values and spirit. I feel this intensely each time I pray at the Kotel in Jerusalem, each time I say the word Jerusalem in my prayers. I am certain you feel this with me.

In building these communities anew, those that rally with us around these values will surely choose to enable construction in lieu of destruction, filling the structures with the meaningful content of these values and this spirit of the People of the Torah through the generations.

We yearn that all of *Am Yisrael* will connect and partner with us in our efforts to build anew.

The Displaced Jews of Gush Katif: Twenty Months Without a Home
By Hillel Fendel on behalf of Arutz Sheva

April, 2007

Over 1,400 former Gush Katif families are living in 26 temporary sites and, for most of them, permanent homes are still a far-off dream.

A report issued by the Gush Katif Residents Committee this month tells the sad, though slowly improving, story:

- Out of 1,667 families expelled from Gush Katif in August 2005 by the Ariel Sharon government, 1,405 are living together in 26 temporary sites. Not one permanent home has begun to be built.

- 284 families, for reasons such as illness or other, have found individual solutions. Many of them plan to rejoin their communities when their permanent homes are built.

- 1,466 families are still seeking communal solutions with their long-time neighbors, according to the following division:

  - 445 are in hotels, tent cities, and yeshiva dormitories, though this number is constantly decreasing.
  - 1,021 are in their medium-term temporary homes, scheduled to remain there for approximately two years, until their permanent homes and communities are ready. The residents say they're far from convinced that it will be only two years. Close to 500 families are living in the prefab community of Nitzan, just north of

Ashkelon, and roughly 200 are in Yad Binyamin, between Ashdod and Beit Shemesh.

- Much of the residents' personal property has been damaged as a result of its storage in large containers. Much property was destroyed and some was even stolen. Many families are having trouble storing it in their new locations.

Agreements

In order to turn a temporary site into a permanent one, a contract must be signed by the government, the temporary residents, and the permanent community or owners already there. Out of the 26 sites mentioned above, only six have signed such agreements.

Preparation for the necessary infrastructure has begun for a third of the families – those living in Nitzan (north of Ashkelon), Bat Hadar (just southeast of Ashkelon), and the Chalutza Sands (Yated and Yevul, due south of southern Gaza along the Israel-Egypt border).

"The reasons for the lack of a contract," the report explains, "differ from place to place – but the bottom-line fact that the state is not finding solutions causes great difficulties and leads to a great lack of confidence, directly influencing other areas of life.

"It is now clear that the caravan sites will be home for the uprooted residents for at least five years."

Promises Unfulfilled

The problems encountered by the government and the residents in their attempt to rebuild their communities are so complex, varied, and time-consuming that they increasingly put the lie to the government's 2005 promise of "a [housing] solution for every resident."

For example, Nitzanim, north of Ashkelon, is now home to 460 families, virtually all of them from five former Gush Katif communities. An agreement to turn the area into a full-fledged town in the framework of the government's flagship project to resettle ex-Gush Katif residents has been signed, but its implementation has been held up by several issues, chiefly that the land was only recently purchased by the government.

The government has also reneged on promises to grant the area preferred status.

Youth

No solution has yet been found for a packing plant to serve the residents' agricultural industries or for an agreed-upon price for land for those expelled Jews who are now coming of age.

This group of displaced Jews, for whom the expulsion was physically, emotionally, and spiritually debilitating, has become known as the "next generation." The full ramifications of the expulsion on these young people, who were approaching the age of military service when they were thrown out from their homes, schools, and communities, has yet to be detailed.

Other would-be communities are waiting for the government to undertake actions such as ordering the Defense Ministry to free up areas currently used for firing ranges, purchasing the promised land, arranging for the budgeting of infrastructure connections, and more.

Regarding schooling, although the Education Ministry is felt to have prepared efficiently for the expelled children, several critical problems have still not been solved. These include school dropout rates that are three times higher than Gush Katif experienced back "at home," as well as the lack of informal education programs, the lack of a satisfactory arrangement for offering social services, and more.

Unemployment

Unemployment was almost unknown in Gush Katif, yet now, 20 months after the expulsion, joblessness stands at 37%.

Around 2,100 Gush Katif residents and others lost their jobs as a result of the Disengagement, including 150 Negev residents and 150 northern Shomron residents. Some 220 people have thus far found jobs, and 50 small businesses have returned to operation. However, owners of independent businesses who have requested to reopen in Nitzan have been turned down, receiving the explanation that small-business structures cannot be placed on the site.

Before the expulsion, the great majority of residents were employed in agriculture, industry, education, and local services, and contributed significantly to the Israeli economy. Of 2,200 who were employed when they lived in Gush Katif, about 400, all of them 50 years of age and over, have essentially given up looking for work.

These 400 were not taken into account when the Employment Bureau recently announced that 75% of

Gush Katif's employees had returned to the work pool.

No State Help

Eligibility for unemployment payments and adjustment funds has long expired. Self-employed workers were never eligible for these funds, and most of them have had no income for the past 18 months.

Some 80 non-agricultural businesses have returned to operation, out of 180, but many of them are in dire straits.

The state decided on a one-time grant to small business owners, but over 85% of those from Gush Katif are not eligible.

Even though the homes of the families of Gush Katif were destroyed, many households continue to pay mortgages – and all of them face increasing expenses related to their relocation – yet more than half of the families have received nothing at all of the promised compensation. The remaining families have received an average of NIS 50,000 (just over $10,000). Only some 5% have received the entire compensation payment.

Due to continued bureaucracy on the part of the Disengagement Administration, the families are expected to produce documentation that is either buried in their storage containers or got lost in the process of the expulsion. "Much of the information demanded by the Administration can be found at the click of a button on other government ministry computers," this report states.

Farmers

Some 30% of the families from Gush Katif ran 400 agricultural businesses, raising tomatoes, celery, flowers, and other crops. Only 33 of these businesses have received land to resume operations.

Out of 176 farmers, 20% have returned to work. Twenty-five people found work independently and 11 were helped by the Disengagement Administration.

The upcoming *shemittah* year, when many religious farmers do not work the land, will mean many Gush Katif refugees will have undergone four consecutive unproductive years, beginning in 2004, when the "Disengagement" was announced, through 2008.

Emotional Difficulties

The displaced families face hardships and psychological pressures caused by financial difficulties, forced unemployment, an uncertain future, loss of community and friends, tight living quarters, bureaucracy, and the like.

The financial compensation provided by the government for new housing is being used by some of the displaced families for day-to-day living. Only 30% of the families have received the full amount, but almost all have received partial compensation.

Some 500 families are aided by welfare organizations. Recent reports indicate that an increasing number of the displaced families are receiving help from government-provided psychological services.

Efforts to implement the Evacuation-Compensation Law have shown its many injustices and unfair restrictions. MKs Uri Ariel (National Union) and Avigdor Yitzchaki (Kadima) are leading a drive in the Knesset to legislate changes and improvements to the existing law. It appears that there is a willingness in the Prime Minister's Bureau to go along with most of the proposed changes.

Caring for One Another

"The situation is wretched, and the state has failed tremendously," said the report, noting that, despite the state's failures, residents of the former communities of Gush Katif are continuing "to work and accomplish."

The report argues that once they receive the necessary tools, and the state can show progress on establishing their permanent communities and improvements in the Evacuation-Compensation Law, "they will once again be an asset to Israel – active, productive, and giving."

This assessment, according to the report, is in no small measure due to the way the residents of the former Gush Katif communities feel and care for each other.

"The communities of Gush Katif are a paradigm of mutual responsibility and concern for the collective. Most of the expellees have remained in the communal framework, hoping to perpetuate their values, ideals, and vision that existed in Gush Katif. Their support for each other is something to be admired," said the report.

According to the report, this has led the community to stand by all its members, especially those who have been considered "ineligible" for whatever reasons by the government.

Communal Life

Even though most of the communities are still located in temporary sites, there have been efforts to maintain a rich communal life.

"The communal strength has greatly enabled them to struggle with the various difficulties – but there are no guarantees. The continuing uncertainty seeps through, and makes every aspect of life more difficult," said the report.

According to the report, the rehabilitation of the displaced Jews from Gush Katif is largely dependent on whether or not the Israeli government grants them a national-priority status, which would include smoothing over the many bureaucratic tangles that must be faced before they can be properly resettled.

"The government must make a comprehensive change in its approach to these problems in order to bring an end to this sad chapter as quickly as possible and ease the difficulties of this sector, which has suffered greatly," said the report.

Laurence Beziz, formerly of Gadid in Gush Katif, is working on behalf of the expelled residents in the Gush Katif-L'maan Acheinu Committee. She explained that most of the body's efforts are now being made in two directions: "Alleviating unemployment, and for the youth, many of whom have fallen through the cracks and are not in school. We are trying to establish a youth club, complete with psychological help and the like. We now have a total number of about 160 youths who are categorized as 'at risk' – about three times higher than what we used to have."

Ms. Beziz emphasized that most residents agree that the extreme extent of the government's failure to help is proof that "they simply want to break us. What the government has done, or failed to do, is much more than mere bungling or ineptitude. Can there be any other explanation for the fact that it took four months to put six measly bus stops here in Nitzan so that our children don't have to wait in the rain to go to school? How else can it be explained that we don't even have one grocery store for the hundreds of families here? There are no basketball courts or normal soccer fields. It was so easy for them to destroy our homes, but they didn't think about how to build up. It is simply criminal and evil."

Asked how people can help, she said, "I can tell you that there is a group from the Jewish communities south of Hebron, such as Susia, that comes here every ten days to volunteer for a few hours and give treatments in reflexology and other methods of alternative medicine. Others have come to volunteer their services in other ways, and some people came to give Torah classes, on Shabbats or during the week – things like these give us encouragement and are very helpful."

About the Authors

Dr. Pesach Aceman is a former resident of Ganei Tal, Gush Katif. He emigrated from Vancouver, Canada in 1973. The diary of his Gush Katif experience was well-documented in the media and was picked up by the BBC which ran it as a regular feature.

Judy Lash Balint is an award-winning Jerusalem-based journalist and writer, and author of *Jerusalem Diaries: In Tense Times* (Gefen, 2002). She is a contributor to the *Peace Fire anthology* edited by Ethan Casey and Paul Hilder (Free Association Books, 2002).

Sara Bedein is a writer and translator who lives with her husband David and their six children in Efrat, Israel.

Rabbi Yosef Elnekaveh was the former Chief Rabbi of Gush Katif. He now lives in temporary accommodation in Yad Binyamin, Israel with his wife and children.

Hillel Fendel is an author and the senior editor and co-founder of Arutz Sheva's "Israel National News." He worked as a teacher and rabbi in the past. Fendel authored a book on prayer entitled *One Thing I Ask*. Published in both Hebrew and English, it contains 180 riddles and questions for readers of all ages on the traditional Jewish prayers.

Michael Freund served as an aide in the Israeli Prime Minister's office to former Premier Binyamin Netanyahu. He is the founder and chairman of Shavei Israel (www.shavei.org), a Jerusalem-based group that reaches out and assists "lost Jews" seeking to return to the Jewish people.

Chaim Gibber is a former resident of Gush Katif. He currently lives with his family in temporary housing in Yad Binyamin, waiting for more permanent relocation. He raises tropical fish.

Rachel Ginsberg writes for Jewish publications in Israel and the United States, and is an editor at *Mishpacha Magazine*. She lives with her family in Beitar.

Toby Klein Greenwald is an educator, a journalist, a photographer, a scriptwriter, and a poet. She has more than 20 years of teaching experience at the college, high school, and elementary school levels, and has served on numerous educational think tanks. In addition to degrees in education, literature, and philosophy, she has studied drama, communications, and graphic art. She is the co-author, together with Dr. Michael Tobin, of a self-help novel on marriage. Toby is married to Jacob and they have six children, two boys and four girls.

Naomi Grossman, originally from London, U.K., has been living in Israel for the past 16 years, during which she has acquired an enduring love of the land. She currently lives in Jerusalem, where she is raising her beautiful family and works as an experienced writer, editor, and translator.

About the Authors

Aaron Klein is World Net Daily's Jerusalem bureau chief. He is known for his regular interviews with Mideast terror leaders and his popular segments on America's top radio programs. His newly released book is *Schmoozing With Terrorists: From Hollywood to the Holy Land, Jihadists Reveal Their Global Plans – to a Jew!*

Esther Marcus lives in Har Nof, Jerusalem with her family. She returned to Israel a month before the expulsion.

Naomi Ragen is an American-born novelist and playwright who has lived in Jerusalem since 1971. She has published seven internationally best-selling novels, and is the author of a hit play.

Sara Yoheved Rigler is a graduate of Brandeis University. Her spiritual journey took her to India and through 15 years of teaching Vedanta philosophy and meditation. Since 1985, she has been practicing Torah Judaism. A writer, she resides in the Old City of Jerusalem with her husband and children. Her articles have appeared in *Jewish Women Speak about Jewish Matters, Chicken Soup for the Jewish Soul,* and *Heaven on Earth.* She has just written a new book, *Lights from Jerusalem.*

Debbie Rosen was a resident of Neve Dekalim for 20 years and has now been relocated with her family to Nitzan. She was a spokeswoman for the Gush Katif movement and spent much of her time shadowing journalists from all over the world.

Rachel Saperstein currently works as a teacher at the Neve Dekalim ulpana. She was a spokeswoman for the Katif Regional Council.

Zimra-Siegman-Schlessinger now lives in the hilltops of Samaria. She works part time as an English teacher and as a Rabbinical Court divorce lawyer. Chananel, Zimra's husband is a *yeshiva* student.

Ami Shaked was a resident of Rafiach Yam and served as the director of the security division of the Katif Regional Council.

Shifra Shomron is a Neve Dekalim, Gush Katif resident-expellee and is the author of the historic novel, *Grains of Sand: The Fall Of Neve Dekalim* (Mazo Publishers, © 2007). "Travel beyond time and beyond location – into my Gush Katif." Visit Shifra's website: www.geocities.com/nevedekalim.

Paula R. Stern is a freelance editor and technical writer. In addition to founding WritePoint Ltd. (www.writepoint.com), she also maintains her personal website (www.paulasays.com) and a site about her son, a soldier in the army, (www.israelisoldiersmother.blogspot.com). She lives in Maaleh Adumim with her husband and five children.

Yehudit Tayar currently lives in Bet Choron. She is a veteran spokesperson for the settlement movement and works closely with the security officers in Yesha and the IDF.

About the Authors

Anita Tucker lived in Netzer Chazani and now lives temporarily in Ein Tzurim. Her grandchildren, who were born in Netzer Chazani, carried a sign as they left home that read, "The Tucker family, 30 years, three generations, this music will continue."

Glossary of Terms

Aliyah
Hebrew. Literally: "Going up." Refers to Jewish immigration to Israel.

Am Yisrael Chai
Hebrew. Literally: "The People of Israel Live."

Amidah
Hebrew. Central prayer recited in each Jewish service. Consists of 19 blessings. Also referred to as the "Shemonah Esrei."

Avodah
Hebrew. Service (of God), currently applied to prayer, previously referring to sacrificial offerings in the Temple.

Bedouin
A sect of Arab nomads who dwell in the desert. Primarily they are located in the Western Desert, Sinai, and Negev to the Arabian Desert.

Bencher
German/Yiddish. Booklet containing the Grace After Meals blessing.

Bereishit
Hebrew. The Book of Genesis. The first book of the Old Testament.

Blood Libel
Sensationalized false allegations that a person or group engages in human sacrifice.

B'nei Yisrael
Hebrew. Literally: "The children of Israel."

Byzantine
The Greek speaking, "Eastern" portion of the divided Roman Empire, conventionally referring to the Middle Ages.

Chessed
Hebrew. Literally: Kindness. Refers to acts of kindness.

Chovot Halevavot
Literally: "Duties of the Heart." Written in Hebrew. Presents ethical and fundamental teachings of Judaism. Written by R. Bachya ben Joseph ibn Paquda.

Chumash
The Five Books of Moses, the *Torah*, from the Hebrew root-word meaning five.

Chuppah
Hebrew. A canopy over the bride and groom. Traditionally used in Jewish weddings.

Daven
German/Yiddish. The act of prayer.

Dunam
Hebrew. Unit of area, approximately 1,000 square meters.

Devarim
Hebrew. The Book of Deuteronomy, the fifth book of the Old Testament.

Erev
Hebrew. The eve of a festival.

Gemara
Aramaic. Literally: "Teaching." Explanations on the *Mishna* or Oral Law, written in Aramaic.

Haftorah
Hebrew. Readings from the Prophets, corresponding to the Torah section. Read in the synagogue on the Sabbath.

Halacha
Hebrew. Jewish law.

Hashem
Hebrew. Literally: "The Name." Used to refer to God.

Hasmoneans
Members of the Hasmonean dynasty, descendants of a priestly family. They led the rebellion against the Hellenist Empire in the second century BCE to establish an autonomous

Jewish Kingdom in Israel. Referred to as 'Maccabees' in the *Talmud*.

Havdalah
Hebrew. Literally: "Separation." Refers to the ceremony following the end of the Sabbath which separates the holy day from the weekday.

Hishtadlut
Hebrew. Literally: "Effort." In reference to meriting Divine help, it is still necessary to make a personal effort.

Kabbalah
Hebrew. "Received" or "Handed Down Tradition." Mystical teachings of the creation and concepts of the spiritual nature of the Universe.

Kaddish
Hebrew. Prayers of sanctification that are traditionally said for the dead.

Kashruth
Hebrew. Dietary laws.

Kedusha
Hebrew. Literally: "Holiness." Communal response, part of the repeated *Amida* prayer.

Ketubah
Hebrew. Wedding contract.

Ketubim
Hebrew. Literally: "Writings." Section of the Old Testament which includes Megillot, Psalms, and Chronicles.

Kiddush
Jewish prayer recited over a cup of wine before a meal on Shabbat or Festivals.

Kiddush Hashem
Hebrew. Literally: "Sanctification of God's name." Referring to self-sacrifice, in effort or of life.

Kippa
Hebrew. Yarmulke or skullcap, male head covering.

Kohanim
Hebrew. Literally: "Priests." Direct male descendants of Aaron, brother of Moses.

Kollel
Hebrew. An institute of advanced studies of *Talmud* and Rabbinic literature for Jewish men.

Kitzur Shulchan Aruch
A popular and condensed version of Jewish Law, compiled by Rabbi Shlomo Ganzfried in the 17th century.

Kriat Shema
Hebrew. Central prayer in Judaism, a declaration of faith. See *Shema*.

Korbanot
Hebrew. Animal offerings and Temple sacrifice mentioned in the *Torah*.

Lamentations
A book of the Old Testament, traditionally read on the festival of *Tisha B'Av*, the fast day that commemorates the destruction of the Temple in Jerusalem.

Lashon Hara
Hebrew. Literally: "Evil tongue." Refers to the Jewish laws that forbid gossip and slander.

Maariv
The evening prayer.

Machnisei Rachamim
Liturgical prayer

Maftir
The last section of the Torah reading that is recited in the synagogue each Sabbath.

Mashiach
Messiah.

Mazal Tov
Hebrew. Literally: "Good luck." Used as a congratulations wish.

Mechina
Hebrew. Literally: "Preparation." Usually refers to a one-year program for post high school children to prepare them for the army or national service.

Megillah
Hebrew. Literally: "Scroll."

Mezuzah
Small parchment scroll with the paragraph of the *Shema* that is affixed to doorposts.

Mikveh
(Plural: Mikva'ot.) A pool of naturally gathered water used for immersing the body for purification.

Mincha
The afternoon prayer.

Mishna
(Plural: Mishnayot.) The written text of the Oral Torah, compiled into six volumes by Rabbi Judah the Prince around 217 CE.

Mitzvah
(Plural: Mitzvot) Divine commandment, or "good deed."

Modim
Part of the *Amida* prayer.

Mukhtar
Arabic. Literally: "Chosen". Refers to the head of a village or group.

Neviim
Prophets. Section of the Bible.

Oneg Shabbat
Hebrew. Literally: "The joy of the Sabbath." Usually refers to a gathering held on the Sabbath with food, singing, and discussion.

Oseh Shalom
Hebrew. Literally: "He Who Makes Peace." A prayer for peace.

Parsha
Hebrew. Weekly portion of the Torah divided into seven sections corresponding to each day of the week.

Pirkei Avot
Hebrew. Chapters of the Fathers; portion of the Mishna dealing with ethical Jewish behavior.

Rebbetzin
Hebrew. The title of a Rabbi's wife.

Sefer Torah
Hebrew. Literally: "Book of Law." The handwritten scroll of the Torah.

Selichot
Hebrew. Penitential prayers usually said in the days before the holidays of Rosh Hashanah and Yom Kippur.

Shabbat
Hebrew. The Sabbath, the Jewish holy day of rest.

Shacharit
Hebrew. The morning prayer.

Shema (Yisrael)
Hebrew. Central prayer in Judaism affirming a belief in one God.

Shemittah
Hebrew. Also called the Sabbatical year. This is the seventh year of the seven-year agricultural cycle mandated by the Torah for the Land of Israel when no agricultural work is permitted.

Shemonah Esrei
Hebrew. See *Amidah*.

Shiur
Hebrew. Literally: "Class." Generally refers to a group meeting to study Jewish texts.

Shiva
Hebrew. Seven-day period of mourning.

Shliach Tzibbur
Hebrew. Messenger/leader of the congregation in prayer.

Shofar
Hebrew. A ram's horn, blown on the Jewish New Year.

Siddur
Hebrew. (Plural: Siddurim.) The Jewish Prayer book.

Sifrei Kodesh
Hebrew. Literally: "Holy books."

Tachanun
A prayer of repentance recited in both the morning and afternoon prayer services.

Talmud
A combination of the *Mishna* and the *Gemara*.

Talmud Torah
Hebrew. (Plural: Talmudei Torah.) Literally: "Learning of the law." The expression denotes a school or class for the study of letters and basic religious texts.

Tefillin
Hebrew:Phylacteries or "frontlets." Black leather boxes containing parchment with quotes from the Torah. Used in the morning prayer, they are strapped on to the arm and around the head.

Tehillim
Hebrew. The Book of Psalms.

Teruma and Maaser
Hebrew. Literally: "Gift and tithes." The laws of separating produce that is grown in Israel.

Torah
Hebrew. The five books of Moses; or Pentateuch, the central text of Judaism.

Tzedaka
Hebrew. Charity.

Tzitzit
Hebrew. Literally: "Fringe." Ritual strings placed on four-cornered garments as commanded in the Torah, a reminder of the 613 commandments.

Viduy/Viddui
Hebrew. Literally: "Confession." The prayer traditionally said before death.

Yarmulke
German/Yiddish. See *Kippa*.

Yehoshua
>Hebrew. The Book of Joshua. The sixth book of the Old Testament.

Yishuv
>Hebrew. Settlement.

www.ingramcontent.com/pod-product-compliance
Lightning Source LLC
LaVergne TN
LVHW011416080426
835512LV00005B/80